Into the twenty-first century:
The development of social security

Into the twenty-first century: The development of social security

A report to the Director-General of the International Labour Office on the response of the social security system in industrialised countries to economic and social change

International Labour Office   Geneva

ISBN 92-2-103631-6

First published 1984

A French edition of this report has been published under the title
La sécurité sociale à l'horizon 2000 (ISBN 92-2-203631-X)

Printed in Switzerland

Preface

Contemporary social security policy has attracted a vast amount
of attention since the current depression shook the complacency
with which most people viewed the future during the steady growth
period of the 1960s. It would seem, however, that the sudden concentration of attention on social security, and in particular on the
legitimacy of state protection, is above all a reaction to current
economic difficulties (increasing unemployment, declining industries, monetary chaos and so forth); and, on these grounds, many
people have not hesitated to accuse social security of aggravating
the world-wide economic crisis.

Certainly, difficult choices will have to be made if society
is to cope with the staggering growth of health care expenditure and
the constant increase in the cost of pensions schemes. However,
there is no point in looking for lasting remedies purely in the light
of the current economic situation: oddly enough, while some social
security deficits make the headlines, stop-gap measures are often
taken which in the long run can only add to the burden of social
expenditure.

To have a sufficiently wide view of an institution like social
security, we need to stand back a little. One tends to lose sight of
the fact that social security, as an essential objective of any modern
society, constitutes a social commitment the true significance of
which cannot be adequately assessed except in the long term: its
workings are part of a process that affect several generations, its
promises have to be fulfilled in a sometimes far distant future, and
individuals will be required to pay contributions throughout their
working lives. Moreover, experience has shown that despite the
rapid transformation of modern societies, social security legislation
and institutions change only slowly, at any rate in essentials.

Since a measure of historical perspective seems necessary
to trace the way ahead, I thought it would be useful to look at what
the future is likely to hold for social security once the present slump
is over. What I had in mind was an examination of the kind of
social security that should be offered to the next generation, or at
any rate a consideration of the solution to the problems that will

arise at the end of the present century. Are we moving towards an overhaul of existing systems in the light of new developments? If so, what do these developments suggest? Along what lines should the matter be pursued?

Such questions deserve a reasoned answer, based on an unshaken belief in a noble cause and looking beyond partisan and narrow-minded short-term considerations. In the discharge of its appointed task and in fulfilment of its responsibility, it was a duty for the International Labour Office to gauge the possibilities, all the more so since for the past half-century the Organisation has endeavoured to guide the development of social security by drawing up international standards which have been at one and the same time a source of inspiration and a guarantee of social progress, and also because it has given its technical support to member States for the creation and development of their social security systems.

I therefore brought together a group of independent experts, whose wide-ranging national and international experience of social security policy, together with their different cultural backgrounds, afforded the maximum guarantee of objectivity and competence. Led by Mr. Pierre Laroque, whose outstanding works have been landmarks in the development of social security studies since the Second World War, the group of ten specialists undertook the formidable task of identifying and analysing the problems and forecasting the social security outlook for the year 2000.

I gave the group precise terms of reference. First of all they were asked to establish the degree of development now attained by social security in the industrialised countries, analysing its achievements and possible shortcomings. Next, they were to draw up a list of questions likely to become important in the future and to indicate, as clearly as possible, the way in which social security systems should develop in order to fulfil the aspirations and requirements of the society of the future in this respect.

Although I asked the group to confine its study to the industrialised countries, I am well aware that the developing countries, too, face formidable social security problems. However, I thought it wiser to limit the scope of this study to a relatively homogeneous group of countries and reserve an analysis of the social security problems of developing countries for a later stage.

After working in complete freedom during several months of consultations and study, the group submitted the result of its work—a detailed report full of questions, observations, ideas and proposals which I have decided to pass on to the public as it stands, whilst at the same time expressing my gratitude to the members of the group for their outstanding achievement.

It will be noted in the first place that the group began by depicting the economic, demographic and social background, against which it set its own specific analysis of the problems of social security. A choice of hypotheses had to be made, since any study of the future has to be founded on options. Whether the hypotheses chosen were valid, only the future can tell: at present there is no rational or objective means of assessing the accuracy of the forecasts of economic growth, demographic trends and unemployment that have been made.

It will also be noted that the group has explored a very vast field. No basic question has been evaded, particularly the present conflict of opinions between people who challenge the objectives and methods of social systems and those who seek, not so much the maintenance of the social benefits already acquired—a relatively static attitude—but that social security should continue to be recognised as one of the fundamental human rights.

Health policy, the social services, cash benefits, financing methods, the role of the private sector in relation to the expected development of the social structure and of individual behaviour are all matters which are analysed with commendable skill and clarity, so that the most complex subjects, however technical they may be, are made to appear easy to understand. The clarity of the text is due to the practised hand of the reporter of the group, Professor Brian Abel-Smith.

The underlying theme of the study flows from the initial statement that in the long term social security has much more far-

reaching objectives than the mere fight against poverty. Social
security must aim at the maintenance of the level and quality of
life and at the strengthening of the individual feeling of security.
Increased prosperity would not justify the progressive dismantling
of social security: quite the contrary. Besides, new fears emerge as
technology evolves. Changes in individual and family behaviour
create new requirements for social solidarity. The experts state,
moreover, that it will not be enough merely to respond to needs as
they arise; it will be necessary to prevent the risks from arising:
hence the importance of preventive measures in the future development of social security systems.

I do not intend to go over again the basic problems dealt
with in the study; to do so would take up too much space, and to
summarise them might be to distort the ideas of the experts or their
close and subtle reasoning. I should nevertheless like to draw the
reader's attention to some aspects of the study, and above all to
my specific purpose in commissioning it.

The recommendations made by the group are aimed at the
persons who have a part to play in the elaboration and implemen-
tation of social security policies and at administrators of social
security institutions. Obviously, the recommendations are not uni-
formly appropriate or pertinent to the national context of each of
the countries of the industrialised world. As the experts have stated
in their foreword, "the priorities of different countries will not be
identical, nor will their capacities to devote further resources to
social security be equal. Our recommendations should be seen as
desirable objectives rather than as mandates which we expect to
be blindly followed irrespective of other considerations and the
cultural values of particular societies."

What is nevertheless a striking feature of the study is the
unanimity shown by the group in its analyses and recommendations. Equally striking is the simple and direct way of treating the
problems considered, far removed from the futurological assumptions or theoretical model-making sometimes found in studies of
this kind.

On the strength of their very extensive experience, the experts do not shrink from rejecting conventional wisdom and challenging a number of shibboleths. The chapter on health programmes illustrates this remarkably. Again, when the experts turn their attention to the need to humanise the administration of social security, they do not mince matters, for instance when they state: "Social security has grown to a vast size in a fog of public ignorance about it. Misunderstandings are widespread and give rise to the exploitation of public prejudices. Social security lacks a base in education at any level and is relatively neglected as a subject for university research"; or again, when they warn administrators that "bureaucratic pressures for efficiency can be carried too far if they result in the depersonalisation of services to users and the neglect of the special needs of minorities".

The experts recognise that the rate of economic growth will determine the rate at which progress can be achieved in the directions they suggest. They are also aware that it will be necessary to choose priorities carefully in order to achieve a balance both within and among various social programmes, and that this will have to be done at each future stage of development. It is, however, satisfactory to note that the group stresses that, in making such choices, attention should first be given to measures benefiting the least favoured sections of society.

The study gives rise to many other reflections.

It reveals that a feeling of security in the face of social risks was long the privilege of a small minority of the population. The machinery of social security has, however, made it possible for the entire population, or at least the great majority, to benefit progressively from the same guaranteed maintenance of their standards and ways of life irrespective of social contingencies. Social security substantially reduces inequality in relation to such contingencies, so that one of the main factors responsible for the distinction between social classes is to a large extent eliminated. Hence the hostility to social security on the part of categories of persons who see the disappearance of what was formerly one of their privileges;

hence also the deep attachment to social security by the mass of the population and their more or less confused awareness of this rise in their social status.

Social security is an instrument for social transformation and progress, and must be preserved, supported and developed as such. Furthermore, far from being an obstacle to economic progress as is all too often said, social security organised on firm and sound bases will promote such progress, since once men and women benefit from increased security and are free from anxiety for the morrow, they will naturally become more productive.

Another impressive aspect of this study is the special attention given to the changes that can be discerned in family life-styles and to the developments that are consequently desirable in the rules governing the provision of benefits. The importance of social security in supporting the family as an agent for the security of its members must not be forgotten. In view of its own objectives, social security should help to strengthen the stability of family ties, such stability being itself a prerequisite for the security of the beneficiaries of the social security system. The demographic component of family policy must also be taken into consideration. By increasing the security of the family, social security will play the active role which I believe it should in support of a population policy.

At another level, the report reveals that the social and, incidentally, economic development made possible by social security is only partially successful as long as it remains the privilege of an élite whilst the mass of the population remain passive beneficiaries. It is therefore essential that these "consumers" of benefits should play an active part in the development process, consciously assuming responsibility for the system from which they benefit.

Their responsibility must stem from a feeling of solidarity. That feeling, which should support all efforts towards social security, needs to be kept alive as the framework within which solidarity is organised becomes larger. There cannot be any social security worthy of the name without the widest national and even international solidarity.

The study is rich in material, and many other reflections could be made. There is one recommendation, however, that cannot fail to lead to questioning and discussion: namely, the introduction of a minimum income for everyone.

Our present social security systems still bear the mark of the traditional Bismarckian reflex and the important legacy of Lord Beveridge. Has the time not come to take up the strands again and establish a coherent set of objectives and methods for the social security of the future, with due regard to the cultural, economic and social conditions of each State?

This may be a forbidding task, but it is also a passionately interesting and necessary one, to which this report will be a valuable contribution. May it lead to reflection, debate and action!

Geneva, 6 September 1983   Francis BLANCHARD
                                           Director-General
                                           International Labour Office

Foreword

We were appointed in late 1980 by the Director-General of the International Labour Office, who asked us to provide him with a report on the likely evolution of social security in industrialised countries as we approach the end of the century. Such a report would analyse broadly the progress made so far by social security in these countries and its alleged shortcomings. It would then identify the questions which are likely to gain prominence in the future and the relative priorities which should be attached to them, with an indication, when possible, of desirable developments in social security provisions.

The recommendations which we make are aimed at those who are likely to influence social security policies and programmes and social security institutions. We appreciate that not every recommendation will be appropriate for each country. Inevitably, the priorities of different countries will not be identical, nor will their capacities to devote further resources to social security be equal. Our recommendations should be seen as desirable objectives rather than as mandates which we expect to be blindly followed irrespective of other considerations and the cultural values of particular societies. The members of the study group were invited to serve in their personal capacities and not as representatives of particular countries or organisations. Yet, despite differences in national background and professional training and experience, we were able to reach a remarkable consensus. As a group we held three full meetings extending over a number of days on each occasion—in April 1981, February 1982 and April 1983. In addition, there have been subgroup contacts and a meeting to work on the text of our report, which we finalised during the April 1983 meeting. Each member contributed material for the consideration of his colleagues, whilst the Secretariat (the Social Security Department of the International Labour Office) placed a wide variety of material and documentation at our disposal; this also helped us considerably in our deliberations.

We wish to thank Mr. Francis Blanchard, Director-General of the ILO, Mr. G. Tamburi, Chief of the ILO Social Security

Department, and the staff of the Department as a whole, for the magnificent support they have given to us throughout the whole period of our work.

Chairman

Pierre LAROQUE,
Président honoraire de la section sociale du Conseil d'Etat,
Paris (France).

Reporter

Brian ABEL-SMITH,
Professor of Social Administration,
London School of Economics and Political Science,
London (United Kingdom).

Members

Miss Ewa BOROWCZYK,
Directeur adjoint,
Institut des assurances sociales,
Warsaw (Poland).

Wilbur J. COHEN,
Sid W. Richardson Professor of Public Affairs,
The University of Texas at Austin (United States),
and formerly
Secretary of the United States Department of Health,
    Education and Social Welfare.

Dr. Jérôme DEJARDIN,
Administrateur général,
Institut national d'assurance maladie-invalidité,
Brussels (Belgium).

John OSBORNE,
Special Adviser Policy Development,
Health and Welfare,
Ottawa (Canada).

António da SILVA LEAL,
Conselho Superior da Acção Social,
Ministério dos Assuntos Sociais,
Lisbon (Portugal).

Adam TRIER,
Deputy Permanent Secretary,
Ministry of Social Affairs,
Copenhagen (Denmark).

Professor Dr. Gérard M. J. VELDKAMP,
Professor of Social Security,
Leiden University,
Leiden (Netherlands).

The Rt. Hon. Sir Owen WOODHOUSE,
President of the Court of Appeal of New Zealand,
Wellington (New Zealand).

Contents

Chapter 7
Summary and recommendations

Chapter 1

The background

1 After a period of unprecedented growth following the Second World War, social security has been increasingly criticised over the past decade. Before we discuss the validity of different types of criticism, it is important to recall the remarkable extensions of social security over the past 40 years. Younger people throughout the industrialised countries take all this for granted. The institutions which now give them such extensive protection against the risks of social and economic life are regarded as an inevitable part of modern life, as the wide security they enjoy is part of the world in which they have grown up. They find it hard to visualise what it meant to live in the circumstances which faced their grandparents. Nor do they face up to what it would cost to support their parents, and possibly also their grandparents as well. In some cases, even grandparents themselves do not remember, or find it convenient to forget, what it was really like in the pre-war years of world depression.

The achievements

2 Over the past 40 years, more and more categories of the population have been brought within the scope of social security, particularly white-collar workers, the self-employed and certain categories of non-employed persons. In some countries, rights have been made universal for certain benefits. One of the important developments is that disabled people are being treated on the same basis in a number of countries, irrespective of the cause of disability.

3 In nearly all highly industrialised countries, cash benefits are now provided for old age, survivors, child support, maternity, unemployment, sickness, prolonged invalidity or disability: health care is provided without charge, or virtually without charge, at time of use. Many countries which did not cover this full range of benefits 40 years ago have extended their provisions to include them. Moreover, within health care, coverage has often been extended to include dental care, ophthalmic care, rehabilita-

tion and specific preventive services. In addition, the duration of
cash benefits has been increased, particularly to cover long-term
invalidity and disability and, in some countries, to give longer protection against the risk of unemployment.

4 Most countries now alter benefits for those not at work so
as to take account of changes in prices, and in some cases
in relation to the growth of earnings of those at work. In some
countries, long-term benefits are related by law to an index; in
others, the authorities use discretionary powers. Moreover, the tendency has been to increase the proportion of earnings replaced by
benefits. Countries which traditionally provided flat-rate benefits
have tended to add earnings-related benefits on top, while countries
with strictly proportional systems of earnings replacement have
tended to establish minimum benefits higher than low-earning beneficiaries would receive by a strict application of the benefit formula. In addition, there has been a growth of complementary insurance (public and private) on top of the basic statutory benefits
and a growth of voluntary membership of statutory programmes
or plans where the rules permit such membership.

5 In some countries, allowances in the income tax for
children have been abolished or reduced, with a corresponding increase in cash allowances for children, on the grounds
that tax allowances gave greater benefits to the higher income
groups and were regarded as inequitable.

6 While in some cases the growth of non-means-tested
contributory or non-contributory benefits has reduced the
traditional role of social assistance, in others relatively generous
provisions for social assistance are available to supplement levels
of benefit which are low. Moreover, there has been a growth of
means-tested benefits which mainly help those in full-time work—
housing allowances or rebates, rate rebates (reductions in property
taxes) and provisions by which those with low incomes are
excluded from social service charges. Some countries have begun

to use negative income tax or tax allowances to help to raise the incomes of the poor.

7   The extent of these developments in social security is indicated by the growth in cost. Narrowly defined (social insurance and assimilated programmes plus family allowances),[1] social security receipts in the OECD countries were within the range of 3 per cent to 12 per cent of gross domestic product in 1960. By the late 1970s, they had risen to between 7 per cent and 23 per cent. For the Eastern European countries, the range was narrower, running in 1977 from 7.5 per cent to 16 per cent of net material product.[2] Under the broader definition of social protection used in the European Community,[3] some countries were spending up to a third of gross domestic product on social security. This is the price which industrialised societies have chosen to pay for the present level of social security. Progress has been gradual as circumstances have allowed, but of course it has always been a considered and deliberate choice. The gain has been in a consciousness of security, even if it is taken for granted, and in the reduction of poverty. Moreover, there is no doubt that the reduction in money barriers in access to health care has contributed to improvements in health and the general quality of life. Younger people today do not ask themselves how they would manage if they had to pay the full cost of bringing up their families, supporting their parents and contributing to the social and health care of their infirm grandparents — and to do all this when their pay stopped the moment they were sick.

8   The extension of social security throughout the 1950s and 1960s was spurred on by a wide political consensus. Different political parties under different political systems all tended to move in the same direction. Criticism of these developments was confined to a small section of public opinion. What, however, is now abundantly clear is that this consensus was built upon economic expansion. When the rate of economic growth declined following the oil crisis of 1973, critics of the expansion of social

security became more vocal. Now some people who attack the
whole basis of social security command a hearing on a scale which
would have been unthinkable ten or 20 years ago. Social security
is criticised for causing adverse economic effects, on the one hand,
and, on the other hand, for failing to fulfil what some now see as
its social purposes.

Adverse economic effects

9 Social security is accused of aggravating the present world-
wide economic crisis. First, it is said to be too costly and
thus a major force contributing to high public expenditure and
unbalanced budgets, leading in turn to high interest rates and low
investment. Second, social security is accused of reducing savings—
the funds available for investment. Third, it is said to add fuel to
inflation. Because of the high taxes and contributions needed to
pay for social security, people are left with too little of their earnings to spend in the way they choose, and thus constantly demand
higher money wages: the resultant inflation causes heavier unemployment. Fourth, social security is blamed for unemployment in
a further way. Where social security is financed by high contributions of employers, the goods produced with artificially increased
labour costs cannot compete on world markets: thus, labour-
intensive production is being handed over to Third World countries
where employers are not burdened with taxes levied on their labour
costs. Moreover, as the return on investment at home is low, funds
are invested abroad. Fifth, social security is accused of damaging
incentives to work both by reducing the rewards for work by the
money raised to pay for it and by what some call the over-generous
compensation paid to those without jobs—whether they are classi-
fied as unemployed, disabled, widows or lone parents. Social
security is said to create the dependency or poverty it is intended
to prevent. Sixth, social security is said to create an excess of
unproductive public sector jobs, crowding out and drawing talent
away from work in the productive private sector.

10 Hence there are some who argue that the way to create jobs and return to previous high rates of economic growth is to dismantle social security—indeed, virtually the whole apparatus of the "welfare state". They concede that governments have responsibilities to help the poor but would confine help to the poor. And they would give the poor cash, not services. Thus both rich and poor would be left to decide for themselves what private insurance they wished to buy. A less extreme proposal would be to provide vouchers (free to the poor and below cost to the near poor) to enable them to choose which packages of services they wished to buy. But both groups would argue that, in our present affluent societies, it is not only wasteful but economically damaging to compel all or nearly all employees and self-employed persons to join state-sponsored or state-run programmes of social security. They believe that most people are in a position to stand on their own feet and make their own decisions about how far they want to protect themselves against the risks of economic and social life.

Failure to achieve social objectives

11 At the same time, social security is attacked for failing to give the adequate security throughout life which its title seems to promise. Despite vast expenditure, social security has failed to solve the whole problem of poverty. More and more countries which had deluded themselves into the belief that poverty had been abolished have rediscovered it. One reason for this is that social security has become so complex and "bureaucraticised" that many people at the bottom of our societies fail to find their way through the maze of entitlements. A second reason is that work-based rights are not extended to those who have never worked. A third reason is that social security tries to draw a hard-and-fast line between the worker and the non-worker. It often fails to provide for those who cannot work a full working day, for those in precarious employment and for those—particularly women, disabled persons and ethnic minorities—on low pay. Finally, it provides inadequately for the family responsibilities of low earners.

12 Second, social security is criticised for discriminating in
the level of benefit it provides according to the cause of
inability to earn, instead of treating people with the same need in
the same way. Persons with equal or identical needs do not get
equal benefits.

13 Third, social security is accused of being created by men
for men and thus of inadequately recognising the responsibilities which society imposes on women. On top of this, it incor-
porates outmoded concepts of dependency and moral judgements,
and penalises those who adopt new life-styles.

14 Fourth, social security is blamed for the fragmentation of
health policy and the promotion of repair medicine, with
only token provision of preventive services; for re-enforcing the
power of service providers; for medicalising social problems (e.g.
treating people in nursing homes who could be at home or in
homes for the aged); and for removing the right of the individual
to take personal responsibility in health matters. Thus, health care
systems are said to be run for the benefit of providers rather than
responding to the aspirations of consumers. Unlike curative health
services, which are generously and often excessively provided,
social welfare services which can make a major contribution to the
quality of life are seriously underprovided.

The underlying tension

15 Social security therefore finds itself today at the centre of
a clash of opinion. It is under fire from both sides. In part,
this is a continuation of an old debate. Politicians and social
security agencies have long had to weigh up the validity of the case
and the strength of the support for those demanding extensions and
improvements in social security against the natural reluctance of
employers, individual contributors and taxpayers to find the money
to finance them. But three features of the debate are new. First is
the weight of criticism from different ideological perspectives of
the failure of social security to meet the needs of the poor or all

the poor. Second is the section of opinion, strong in some countries and weak or non-existent in others, challenging the whole framework upon which social security has been built. Third is the view that in many countries it is no longer possible to finance improvements in social security out of economic growth and still leave those who ultimately bear the cost with rising real cash incomes. Indeed, in a number of countries, cuts in the living standards of the majority have been imposed simply to meet existing commitments as they unfold on top of other commitments of the public sector.

16 It is this last fact which has created the present tension. And the tension has contributed to the instability of political coalitions and the collapse of governments before their normal term. Public opinion has found it difficult to come to terms with the new economic realities. Governments which try to modify, qualify or remove social security rights in the hope of reducing inflationary pressures encounter strong resistance. Those which do not are faced with criticism of the level of tax and contributions and strong inflationary pressures. It has not been easy for the public to come to terms with the arithmetic of a zero sum game following over two decades of more of everything. It is now abundantly clear, as mentioned earlier, that the wide consensus favouring the expansion of social security during the 1950s and 1960s and extending into the 1970s was built upon economic expansion. During this period the growth of social security throughout the world was vast and without precedent. More people were covered for more risks, and benefits tended to become relatively more generous. Before we turn to the future, it is right to acknowledge what has been accomplished. From the point of view of the beneficiaries, social security has real achievements to its credit in increasing the scope of the protection provided.

The rise in the cost

17 The cost of social security has been rising for the obvious reasons that more people have been covered for a wider

range of benefits and that in many countries the level of benefits
has risen faster than average net earnings (after the payment of tax
and social security contributions). But on top of this there are further reasons for the rising cost which are not so widely understood:

1. *The maturing and development of programmes.* Many retirement
   pension programmes have been steadily maturing. The newly
   aged have acquired more generous rights than the elderly. Similarly, people who have become disabled recently have more generous rights than people who became disabled 10, 20 or 30 years
   ago, and in some countries these higher rights have been
   extended to those disabled earlier.

2. *Social and demographic change.* The ageing of the population
   in all industrialised countries has greatly increased both expenditure on pensions and expenditure on health care, as the aged
   generally use two or three times more health care than those of
   working age. In most countries, this trend is continuing. More
   people have been retiring earlier. In some countries, the right to
   retire early, with the aim of releasing jobs for younger people,
   has added further to the cost of pensions. On top of this the
   growth of one-parent families has imposed heavy burdens,
   mainly on systems of social assistance. While, in some countries,
   the trend towards a higher proportion of aged to the population
   of working age has reached its maximum, within the aged the
   proportion of over-75s who make such heavy demands on health
   and social services has been steadily increasing.

3. *The rising cost of health care per beneficiary.* Technological
   developments in medicine, increased specialisation, higher standards of amenity and care, wider demands of beneficiaries and
   increased relative pay and fringe benefits and shorter working
   hours for persons working in health care systems have all added
   to the cost of health care provided to beneficiaries in all age
   groups.

4. *Unemployment.* Of critical importance has been the trend in the
   industrialised market economy countries during the 1970s and

early 1980s towards much higher levels of unemployment than
were experienced in the 1950s or 1960s. This has increased the
cost of unemployment benefits tremendously and has placed
massive burdens on social assistance systems after rights to these
benefits have been exhausted. While the growth of unemployment has brutally increased the cost of social security programmes, it has at the same time cut down their income by
reducing the number of contributors and the yield of taxes.

18 It may be expected that the cost will continue to increase
faster than national resources up to and beyond the year
2000, for the following reasons:

(a) in the changing demographic structure of most industrialised
countries, the proportion of the aged is increasing;

(b) pension programmes are still maturing;

(c) the proportion among the aged of elderly persons who make
such heavy demands on health and social services is bound to
increase still further;

(d) technological progress in medicine is continuing, and so is the
medicalisation of social problems; and

(e) the vast expansion of medical education is leading to a rapid
increase in the number of doctors, which will greatly increase
costs.

On top of this there is a whole shopping list of new demands for
improvements and extensions from spokesmen for particular categories of beneficiary and potential beneficiary. On the other hand,
there are clear signs of resistance from those who see themselves
in the capacity of contributor rather than of beneficiary. And this
raises the question of which groups in society are lending their support to those who want to see the role of social security curtailed
or even the whole system dismantled and recast. How far are
employers making the social security system the scapegoat for the
world recession? How far are those with higher pay and secure
employment blaming the victims of radically changed economic

circumstances? How far are those who work hard for low pay
expressing their resentment that so many people should get nearly
as much for doing nothing at all? Whatever the answers to these
questions, the tensions in society are a political fact. How are the
conflicting pressures to be resolved in the long run?

Some of the questions to be answered

19 Is it true, as some critics assert, that the burden of social
security costs is damaging economic progress? If it is, can
a less damaging way of financing it be found? If social security
costs should be cut or constrained, on which benefits should the
axe fall? Should we be moving towards higher pension ages,
towards steadily increasing cost-sharing in health care, or towards
restricting or freezing pensions and benefits in current money terms
so that any further provision should be made by investment in the
private sector? What should be the long-term relationship between
the private sector and the public sector? Are people becoming so
affluent that the whole fabric of social security can be steadily dismantled except for some residual provision for the poor?

20 These are some questions which, under our interpretation
of our terms of reference, we are required to answer. Social
security has been presented to those who benefit from it as a long-
term commitment. Thus, if fundamental changes are required, they
should only come gradually and must be planned and notified to
beneficiaries long in advance. This we interpret to be one of the
reasons why our terms of reference require us to look so far
ahead—up to the year 2000.

Underlying assumptions

21 But we are also asked to consider what economic and social
changes are likely to influence the need for social security
provision up to the year 2000, and to recommend the type of response which social security should make to adjust to these new
developments.

22 Of central importance is the assumption made about long-term economic prospects. Are we to assume a perpetuation of the present economic scenario of low or nil growth and heavy unemployment in the highly industrialised countries? Or are we to assume, at the other extreme, an eventual resumption of economic growth on the scale of that of the 1950s and 1960s which will steadily mop up the present unemployment and lead to still greater participation of married women in the working population, to shorter annual working hours and thus to the need for a greater emphasis on preparation for and the use of leisure?

23 For the purpose of this report, the view we take is midway between these extreme positions. We are optimistic enough to believe that in the long term a way will be found to increase productivity and reduce unemployment substantially, though the process may be slow and uneven. The impact of the multiplier upwards should not be underestimated once the process has acquired sufficient momentum. We believe this because the present situation is essentially irrational. Though a tendency to a higher level of unemployment could be detected in the 1960s and early 1970s, it was the sudden increase in the price of oil in 1973, repeated in 1979, that provoked what was then a severe imbalance in trade between oil-producing and other countries. The longer-term impact has been to stimulate the search for further sources of oil, for ways to save fuel and for alternative sources of energy. These efforts are beginning to produce results. There is no longer the same imbalance of trade. We are aware that some are arguing that the growth of new technology is bound to lead to heavy unemployment in the long run. But historical experience shows that, in the past, technological developments were in time absorbed. We expect this to happen again. Essentially they are a way of raising living standards and thus making possible higher real incomes from shorter annual working hours and more flexible work patterns, such as sabbaticals and periods of part-time work at the employee's choice. Work in the future may be very different from work today.

24 But the question which is often asked is where new jobs are likely to be created. As we see it, the potential for growth in the service and leisure industries is virtually unlimited. Among the service industries are those which promote health and social welfare. With a resumption of economic growth, people will be prepared to pay more for these services. Developments in social security could help to overcome the present crisis of unemployment if acceptable means could be found for financing it or if the psychological resistance to paying could be overcome.

25 Thus the long-term future which we are assuming is one with substantially higher levels of employment and with a resumption of growth, though not at the rate of the 1950s and 1960s. This assumption about growth is of critical importance for women as well as men. Our assumption that a high proportion of growth will be concentrated in the service and leisure industries augurs well for job opportunities for women, even given the existing division of jobs between the sexes. But we also assume that there will be a reduction in sex discrimination in employment opportunities, and that women will be less sex-role-typed by education, training and social convention in the jobs they seek. This is as essential for the promotion of social security in its widest sense as it is for the proper recognition of human rights. Finally, we assume that greater equality in job opportunities will be accompanied by a greater degree of sharing of household and parental roles. All this has major implications for social security.

26 The steady replacement of men by machines is likely to lead to changes in the composition of the labour force. More people with very high skills and professional training will be needed in industry. There will still be a need for people with limited training or education, but there will be a steady decline in the demand for those with moderate skills. In service occupations, however, there will still be room for skills at every level. This again is of special importance for women. In the future, continuing education will be even more important than in the past. Social security will have greater importance as a force which helps to integrate individuals and groups in society, by seeing that basic needs are met, by securing a fairer distribution of resources and by extending the supply of services—including those geared towards self-development, self-expression and the use of leisure. But social security will need to offer more personalised services to offset the negative effects of computerised standard information and retrieval systems. We discuss this issue in Chapter 5.

27 Over the past 20 years there has been a trend towards new life-styles. While marriage as a social institution has continued to be the norm, separation and divorce have become much more frequent. A significant and growing proportion of men and women now marry more than once in a lifetime. Cohabitation before marriage and between marriages has become much more common. And some enter into cohabiting relationships without the sharing of income assumed in a quasi-marital relationship. As a result of all these trends, there are at any time more one-parent families. There are, moreover, new patterns of dependency when two persons live together for long periods, though one party to the relationship may be the major earner or sole earner.

28 It is impossible to predict whether the trend towards these new life-styles will continue or whether there will be a return to older values reinforced by social sanctions. But social security must be ready to adapt to these new social patterns.

29 Somewhat less speculative are the demographic trends. It is not possible to predict whether the present low birth rates (which are below replacement rate in a number of countries) will continue. But it seems right that social security should continue to lighten the financial burden of parenthood and in some countries should reinforce this policy. On the other hand, it is clear that most industrialised countries will be faced with a higher proportion of persons over 65 and all will have a higher proportion of elderly

(over 75) in the year 2000. The majority of them will be women and the majority will be persons living alone. Their rights to pension will derive from their own or their partner's working life which ended ten or substantially more years ago.

30 In this connection, the future trends in prices and real earnings are of special relevance. However desirable it would be to return to long-term price stability, it would be extremely rash for social security to be planned on this assumption. Thus it is assumed that inflation will continue at rates which cannot be predicted in advance. As mentioned earlier, we are assuming a modest growth in real wages.

31 These are the key assumptions which underlie our report. It is not our task to map out a future which we would consider desirable—whether on moral, social or economic grounds— but simply to recognise those trends to which social security will need to adapt. But this does not mean that we envisage a wholly passive role for social security. On the contrary, later in our report we lay great stress on prevention and rehabilitation. But, ultimately, social security must provide for contingencies which have not been prevented.

32 In Chapter 2 we define the aims of social security for the period up to 2000. In Chapter 3 we work out the implications of these aims in cash benefits and, in Chapter 4, in services. We devote Chapter 5 to relations between social security institutions and the public. In Chapter 6 we discuss the financing of social security. Our conclusions are summarised in Chapter 7.

Notes

   [1] Social insurance and assimilated schemes plus family allowances are defined for this purpose as systems of social security covered by the series of inquiries into the cost of social security initiated by the ILO after the Second World War, with the exception of systems for public workers (both military and civilian), public health services, means-tested systems and benefits in respect of war victims. For further details, see ILO: *The Cost of Social Security: Tenth International Inquiry, 1975-1977* (Geneva,

1981), Introduction: "Scope of the inquiry" and notes attached to the comparative tables.

[2] Net material product is defined as the total net value of goods and productive services (including turnover taxes) produced by the economy. (By productive services or material services are understood services such as transport, commodity circulation, storage, etc., which are considered to be a continuation of material production). See United Nations, Department of Economics and Social Affairs, Statistical Office: *Yearbook of National Accounts Statistics, 1979* (New York, 1980; Sales No. E.80.XVII.11), Vol. I, p. xvii, and earlier issues.

[3] Any expenditure involved in meeting costs incurred by individuals or households as a result of the materialisation or the existence of certain risks, contingencies or needs, in so far as this expenditure gives rise to the intervention of a "third party, without there being any simultaneous equivalent counterpart by the beneficiary". See Statistical Office of the European Communities: *European system of integrated social protection statistics (ESSPROS): Methodology — Part I* (Luxembourg, Office for Official Publications of the European Community, 1981), Ch. 2, para 206.

Chapter 2

Objectives for the year 2000

Historical evolution

__33__ In most highly industrialised countries, social security policy has passed through three stages. First was an era of paternalism: private charity and public poor relief provided for the poor, being often subject to harsh conditions which imposed stigma. Second was an era of social insurance: following the precedents of friendly societies and of pensions and sick pay for employees in public and some private occupations, wider compulsory programmes were developed covering more and more occupations and more and more contingencies. In some countries, the occupational origin of social security is still retained in the form of separate funds. In the third stage the concepts of prevention and universality have begun to be incorporated and the range of services is being extended with the aim of maintaining and enhancing the quality of life of families and individuals. The stages are not clear cut: more than one stage of development may be found in the same country at the same time.

__34__ Social insurance was a somewhat related recognition that, particularly in wage-earning industrialised and urban societies, individuals and families could not be expected to provide for their own security. In some countries, protection against the risk of occupational accidents and, later, sickness was the first to be provided. Pensions were a response both to the growing practice of retirement and to the desire to reward loyal service, and widows' benefits were a recognition of the rights of married women. But the experience of the economic depression between the world wars gave a major boost to social security policies. It was proved beyond doubt that lack of a job could not simply be blamed on the individual. Long-term unemployment removed the ability of these individuals to save and insure for the other risks of social and economic life. Social insurance was seen as a force which not only gave security to those covered but could help to give greater stability to unstable economic systems.

35 We see it, therefore, as paradoxical that the whole rationale of social security should come to be questioned at a time when so many highly industrialised countries are faced with unemployment on a scale which has not been experienced for 40 to 50 years, when many workers are being forced into early retirement and when marriage break-up has replaced widowhood as the major traumatic risk facing married women with family responsibilities which have prevented them from participating in the world of work. It is beyond doubt that there has been no period since the aftermath of the Second World War when the need for effective social security policies has been greater. Moreover, today unemployment falls disproportionately on the young, the unskilled and immigrants. It falls on those who are least likely to own a home, to have acquired consumer durables or to have had a substantial working life during which savings can be accumulated.

36 In its historical origin, social insurance has had different rationales in different societies. In some countries, it was designed with the simple aim of maintaining income—of giving security. Measures to combat poverty were seen as a separate field of social policy. However, as mentioned earlier, some earnings-related plans have since developed minimum benefits greater than a strict application of the benefit formula would warrant. Thus an element of redistribution has been incorporated. In so far as poverty was reduced, it was in the case of those defined contingencies for which social security provided.

37 In other countries, social insurance evolved as a non-stigmatising means of combating poverty. Benefits were originally flat-rate and later included additions for dependants. Such was the Beveridge concept developed in the United Kingdom, which had a considerable influence on world developments. Many flat-rate programmes have since developed an earnings-related tier above them, but the intention has been to retain an element of redistribution towards the poor. But the world influence of Beveridge was greater in terms of his emphasis on universal health care and family allowances.

38 Social insurance and the universal provision of benefits (such as pensions or family allowances) are only two of the mechanisms which provide cash as part of policies for social security. Social assistance and means-tested benefits back up, and in some cases supplement, social insurance benefits. And more recently income tax has come to be used in some countries as an instrument of social security policy, through special allowances (e.g. for health care costs or health insurance) or a system of negative income tax. On the other hand, in some countries income tax as well as other taxes (including social security contributions) can be a cause of hardship where the threshold of taxation is below the poverty line. We discuss these problems in Chapter 6.

The aims of social security

39 As we see it, social security has wider aims than the prevention or relief of poverty. It is the response to an aspiration for security in its widest sense. Its fundamental purpose is to give individuals and families the confidence that their level of living and quality of life will not, in so far as is possible, be greatly eroded by any social or economic eventuality. This involves not just meeting needs as and when they arise but also preventing risks from arising in the first place, and helping individuals and families to make the best possible adjustment when faced with disabilities and disadvantages which have not been or could not be prevented. Thus social security requires not only cash but also a wide range of health and social services, which we discuss in Chapter 4. It is the guarantee of security that matters most of all, rather than the particular mechanisms, such as contributory or tax financing, the insurance or service model of delivery, or the ownership of facilities (public/private, profit/non-profit) by which that guarantee is given. Considerations of economic efficiency and participation, national tradition, user acceptability and the availability of particular insti-

tutions may point towards particular mechanisms in particular
societies. But the means should not be confused with the ends.

40 Over the years there has been a trend towards universal
coverage, and more and more risks have come to be recognised and provided for. They include maternity benefits and family
benefits. But in many countries there are still risks which can seriously threaten income security and which should eventually be
recognised, but for which inadequate provision has so far been
made. In most countries, the provisions made for those with family
responsibilities are underdeveloped. And often there is inadequate
protection against the risk of reduced earning capacity because of
ageing or partial disability. The extent to which and the circumstances in which legal costs are met varies between countries: the
right to justice can be no less important than the right to health
care, even though the risk is of less common occurrence. Similarly,
the costs of particular types of education and training for mature
students may have to be met at the cost of a sharp fall in living
standards. In many countries, there are no safeguards against arbitrary eviction from housing or a family farm, or against arbitrary
dismissal by an employer or the bankruptcy of the employer—all
of which can involve major threats to security. These are all risks
for which social security provision should logically be made in
some form. Another form of insecurity arises where people are
living on credit to the extent that even a small drop in income (e.g.
the lack of opportunities for overtime, or crop failure) can mean
that they are unable to meet both their minimum needs and the
rate of repayment plus interest for which they have contracted.
While these problems can be eased in a number of ways through
social security, we see no way in which social security can be
adapted to solve them all completely.

41 But it has increasingly been recognised that the prevention
or reduction of risk, where this is possible, is the better way
of providing security. Thus, legislation may be used to give protec-

tion against arbitrary eviction from a home or a farm or arbitrary dismissal from a job. Preventing accidents and ill-health, originally arising from the job but now in their widest sense, is to be preferred to the provision of curative and social services and cash benefits. Rehabilitation is to be preferred to the provision of continuing benefits for partial or total incapacity to work. Protection against unemployment by employment maintenance and promotion, by job creation and job subsidy, by retraining those with redundant skills, by assisting the mobility of the workforce and by resettling the unemployed, is to be preferred to the replacement of lost income. These developments require the close co-ordination of a wide range of policies and services to find the best solution for the individual and the family.

42 As pointed out in Chapter 1, the coverage of social security has been rapidly expanded over the last 40 years. Some countries now provide tax-financed benefits to all residents. In others, health services and/or family allowances and pensions for the aged are provided to all residents, while other benefits are limited to those who have paid contributions. Some benefits, such as unemployment benefits, do not extend for the whole period for which the contingency lasts. Gaps are filled by social assistance, but not in all circumstances in all countries. We *recommend* as a central aim that persons not currently protected or inadequately protected should be fully covered where it has not been possible to prevent the contingency or its continuance. This latter is obviously the preferable solution.

Does greater affluence justify dismantling?

43 In a richer society, should individuals be left to make their own arrangements? Can the role of compulsory social security be reduced as societies become more affluent? All the arguments point in the reverse direction. First, it is clear that growing affluence has produced further insecurities—particularly those of redundant skills—and has been accompanied by social changes such as the much greater rate of break-up of marriages. Second, there are risks for which full insurance cannot, in practical terms, be purchased on the private market: unemployment and the long-term costs of health and social care. Nor can insurance provide for the economic consequences of marriage break-up or having a large family. This has important implications for the ability to continue to pay for pensions and other benefits. Third, because of earlier retirement and longer survival, the cost of pension insurance has been rising faster than national income per head. Fourth, the cost of health insurance has also been rising faster than national income per head. Over the past 40 years every industrialised society, irrespective of political system or the predominant political party in power, has in fact increased the range of benefits covered, and generally the relative level of income replacement. As a question of fact, the higher income groups are in general more fully insured than the lower income groups, often through company plans. The development of social security has not led to the demise of voluntary savings and private insurance, as some argued it would. Substantial savings and insurance continue on top of social security provision among all income groups, and particularly the higher income groups. On average, people seek greater security, the more they have to preserve. To compel people to insure, who fail to recognise or provide for the risks that face them, becomes no less important as a society becomes more affluent. Even in such societies there are people who cannot afford to insure.

44 It should also be emphasised that, quite rightly in this modern age, social security has a strong legal basis. The right to it is not only included in many national constitutions but is also contained within the Universal Declaration of Human Rights. Most countries have endorsed the Declaration of Philadelphia, adopted by the International Labour Conference in 1944, and ratified a number of international labour Conventions, particularly the Social Security (Minimum Standards) Convention, 1952 (No. 102).

Can income-tested benefits replace universal benefits?

<u>45</u> Universal benefits contribute to a nation's sense of community and interdependence—to national solidarity. Income-tested benefits tend to be kept low because of the attitudes of non-beneficiaries. The attempt to use an income-tested benefit to eliminate the gap between the poor who are not at work and those who earn low wages can be seen as an attempt to extinguish relative rewards which have been earned by the latter, and can lead to inflationary wage claims to restore the pre-existing gap.

<u>46</u> The argument—that, if the better-off were left to buy their own insurance, more generous provision could be made for the poor on an income-tested basis—seems at first sight to have a compelling logic. But people are much more willing to contribute to a fund from which they derive benefit than to a fund going exclusively to the poor. The poor gain more from universal than from income-tested benefits. There is, moreover, some limited empirical evidence to support this assertion. Income-tested benefits can be damaging to incentives to work and save, and certainly penalise those who do so. Moreover, many countries already have (in addition to universal income maintenance programmes) social assistance programmes, income-tested housing allowance, food stamps, rate rebates and a whole range of provisions by which the lowest income groups can obtain particular services free, for which those better off have to pay. Already many countries are faced with a problem of a poverty trap: earning more leads to little more to spend, because other benefits and allowances are reduced as income rises. In these countries, there is simply no room for a further large income-tested programme in addition to existing income-tested programmes without totally destroying the incentive to work. A negative income tax cannot be accommodated because the space for it is already filled by other programmes. Moreover, virtually all income-tested programmes suffer from problems of failing to claim. For this reason, they do not reach all the poor.

47 The withdrawal of universal benefits would rapidly lead to a growth of company-based schemes to serve a similar function. The extent of provision would be greatest in companies with a strong position in their markets. Some companies, particularly small ones, would make no provision at all. Thus the dual labour market would be reflected in provisions for security. The worker with precarious employment, intermittent employment and casual employment would have his insecurity of work reflected in a grossly inadequate provision for sickness, disability and old age. Moreover, in so far as the cost of the fringe benefits paid in the powerful companies could be passed on in higher prices, the worker without security would be contributing to the cost of provisions for those with the advantage of secure employment.

48 Those who argue that it is wrong for legislation to compel people to insure, because they should have the right of individual choice, see no objection to employers thrusting insurance on their employees. Thus the argument is not about whether there should be social security but about its coverage and who should decide it. It is essentially an argument about national solidarity.

49 Social insurance benefits provide a foundation on which special income-tested programmes can be built to meet particular needs. A substantial right to cash without a test of income can be supplemented by a programme which secures a national minimum on a selective basis, taking account of the special circumstances of particular families. The particular mechanism for securing this minimum will need to vary according to the pattern of arrangements in each country. We discuss this further below. But the existence of a generalised right to social security providing a limited level of benefits makes it easier to construct an income-tested programme without damage to incentives to work and save.

The level of cash benefits

50 What level of benefits is needed to ensure that levels of living are not greatly eroded by social and economic even-

tualities? As mentioned earlier, there is a trend towards a convergence of benefit formulas. Earnings-related supplements enforced by legislation are being built above flat-rate benefits, and minimum benefits are being built into earnings-related formulas. It is noticeable that it is where flat-rate benefits are relatively low in relation to earnings that earnings-related supplementation tends to be statutory. It is, however, wrong to imagine that flat-rate benefits always are low.

51 The case for earnings-related benefits is that they recognise the rewards of skill and reflect customary levels of living. Furthermore (as we said in paragraph 46), once such a system is in operation it is likely to receive much wider acceptance from those who are to contribute, since they themselves may expect protection of their own living standards. In that situation they can, of course, be taxed on a similar basis to income from work. Already this general approach has been given legislative support in many countries. We *recommend* accordingly, and we believe, that at least a significant element of earnings-related benefit is desirable.

52 In some countries it may seem acceptable to leave earnings-related provision to private negotiation between the social partners when a high level of flat-rate benefits is provided by a general programme. The weaknesses, however, of private plans are that pensions are not effectively portable between employments, that employers' contributions are normally not vested until a worker has attained a certain age and completed a certain length of employment, that workers can withdraw their own contributions on changing jobs, that some plans do not remain solvent on the bankruptcy or takeover of the firm, that it is difficult for pensions to be fully indexed against inflation, and that those who change jobs during their working life derive less than they deserve from pension formulas which relate pension to salary on retirement. In the case of private pension plans, therefore, there are clear advantages in moving towards coverage of whole industries rather than coverage within individual firms. We *recommend* that private pension plans should be required to shift in this direction in order to improve arrangements for the transfer of pension rights between plans, or for the full protection of acquired rights and plan solvency, and that they should include some element of inflation protection for pensions in payment to be built into such plans. Thus we *recommend* that private pension plans should be regulated with these ultimate aims in view.

53 We *recommend* that the long-term aim should be to ensure that the minimum benefits paid to those not at work should provide a level of living of at least half the average net disposable income per head. By net disposable income, we mean income, adjusted for families of different composition, that is received after tax and social security contributions have been paid. The level of benefit needed to secure this will depend on whether it is taxed and whether any social security contributions have to be paid. We recognise that the minimum level of social security benefits has implications for minimum wage legislation: in general, the minimum income replacement benefit for a single person should not exceed the minimum wage for that person.

Indexing for inflation or growth

54 Long-term social security benefits or pensions fail to protect living standards unless they are indexed. In a period of economic growth, relating pensions to prices is inadequate: pensioners have a right to share in rising national prosperity to keep their relative place in the society in which they live. Thus we *recommend* that pensions in payment should be related to an index of earnings or of gross domestic product per head to allow for unemployment and demographic change. Minimum pensions should, however, be related to average earnings as above.

55 It is often argued that indexing pensions adds to inflation. The short answer is that indexing pensions does no more than maintain for pensioners their share of the national product. If pensions are related to the growth of the economy, pensioners cannot be blamed for receiving more than is warranted by the increase in national productivity. In such matters pensions have by definition a passive role. We see no justice in singling out pensioners as a particular group in society who are forced to suffer for the inflation caused by others.

The battle against poverty

56 As mentioned above, many social security programmes were not designed with the central aim of reducing, let alone eliminating, poverty, except in the case of the identified categories for which provision was made. The vertical distribution of income was taken as given, and reflected in the benefits. Thus it is hardly relevant to criticise them for failing to achieve the objective of eliminating poverty, which they were never set. Where social security programmes did have as an objective the fight against poverty, the effort was mainly concentrated on those not at work: family allowances and health services were the only instruments used to help those who were at work.

57 But now that the aim of social security has been widened to include the promotion of the whole quality of life, and now that coverage is approaching the whole resident population, should the objective of fighting poverty be explicitly incorporated as one of the central aims of social security policy?

58 All of us agree that the persistence of poverty is unacceptable in affluent societies, though one member of our group believes that the introduction of a general standard minimum income as part of a system of social security would be highly undesirable for the following reasons. First, basic needs vary according to age, health, rural or urban living and other individual and family circumstances. No standard minimum could provide for all these different requirements. Second, drawing a hard-and-fast line between the poor and non-poor involves discrimination and segregation, which is socially and psychologically damaging and is likely to generate antagonism between the two groups—those who see themselves as paying, and those who are seen as the main recipients of payments. Such a division is likely to encourage the non-poor to blame the poor for their poverty. Moreover, in so far as a battle against poverty would require further means-testing, this is undesirable and those administering social security programmes should not be put into the position of having to inquire about incomes. Third, this member believes that provision of a minimum would absorb a disproportionate and growing share of resources at the expense of the main aim of providing security, and that this would lead eventually to the erosion of the whole social security system. Social security has been built and promoted on the idea that the need for provision for security is applicable to all socio-economic groups. A national minimum would undermine this sense of national solidarity which has been carefully fostered over the years.

59 The rest of us do not accept these arguments. In our view, the establishment of a minimum does not exclude the possibility of supplementation by social assistance in individual cases according to special needs. If the incentive to work is to be preserved, there will inevitably have to be some sort of tapering in the provision of a minimum income, as, for example, with the allowances for housing operative in many countries. Thus there would not be any hard-and-fast division between the poor and the non-poor. The cost will depend on the level of the minimum and the extent of taper, but we do not believe it would be impossibly large. Nor would it be in competition solely with funds for social security. Compared with the current cost of maintaining such a large number of unemployed, it would not impose an impossible burden to find the money as the world climbs out of the present recession. Finally, a national minimum is seen by the majority of us as a further development of national solidarity rather than as any erosion of this vital principle.

60 In the view of the majority, a national minimum is essential to meet what should be regarded as the first and cer-

tainly an imperative challenge for any good system of social
security: the responsibility for the disadvantaged and the under-
privileged. Where people are deprived of income, decent housing
and a decent environment, opportunities to participate fully in the
life of the country in which they live and, above all else, are
deprived of self-respect, they cannot be said to be experiencing an
acceptable quality of life. Poverty is multi-dimensional and so normally are its causes. We are not arguing that a minimum income
is a "solution" to the problem of poverty. A whole battery of services is needed to help different groups of poor people to become
full participating members of society. But a minimum income
should be provided with other forms of help, when such help is
appropriate. We are well aware that, in bringing anti-poverty policy
into the mainstream of social security policy, we are arguing for a
major widening of the field. Services which can help to reduce poverty include health services, housing services, education and
training services and employment services. People can be poor in
terms of health, education, employment and other services available and accessible to them. But of central importance is cash. The
majority *recommend* that building an effective minimum income
for all residents should be accepted as the major challenge for social
security policy to be achieved before the year 2000.

61 We have defined above the minimum level of income for
those not at work. The majority intend this minimum to
apply to all: those who are mentally retarded, who are congenitally
disabled or who have become disabled before entering the labour
force, one-parent families headed by a parent who has never been
in the labour force, adults entering the labour force or in training.
The minimum is also intended to apply to those working part-time
or on short-time, to those whose working capacity has been reduced
by partial disability, to casual workers and the self-employed. But
we would exclude those on strike or in full-time education. Separate
provision may be made for the latter on different terms. It is not,
however, intended that the right to a minimum income should be

individualised. Married couples have an obligation to maintain each other. When there are quasi-marital relations, difficult problems may arise. It is necessary to avoid creating an inducement for families to split up. As mentioned earlier, a work incentive will need to be built into the programme. A minimum level of income could be phased in, starting with categories where this last problem does not arise and then bringing in those whose social need is greatest. First could be the aged and disabled and those needing residential care. Second could be families with dependent children, on the grounds that children must not be deprived of opportunities for growth and development equal to those in more affluent families. Third might be persons undergoing retraining before seeking placement in new jobs.

62 The mechanisms used to achieve an effective minimum will vary between countries. Minimum wage legislation and an adequate level of family allowances with extra provision for one-parent families can ease the problem. But the minimum will certainly be on a selective basis, taking account of not only income but also realisable assets. In some countries, it may be built upon rent allowances, with special provisions for home owners or purchasers; in others, it may be based on subsidised services. In still others, refundable tax credits or reverse income tax may be used. Different mechanisms may be used for different groups of the population. And other means-tested programmes may need adjustment to accommodate the new structure of the minimum.

63 Difficult decisions will need to be taken not only about the definition of the family unit but also about what assets should be regarded as realisable for this purpose, how income should be defined, what income should be disregarded for work incentive or other reasons, what accounting period should be chosen, and so on. A balance will have to be struck between a system which is so invasively inquisitive that it fails to reach a substantial number with the right to claim and a system which permits an element of rough justice and tolerates a certain amount of abuse. None of these problems is readily resolved. This is why this aim is presented as a challenge, for this is what it is. But we repeat that, despite disagreement about mechanisms, we all regard the persistence of poverty as intolerable in affluent societies which have both the resources and the potential administrative skill to remove it, if they have the political will to do so.

Movement between countries

64 A further cause of loss of security which is not fully provided for at present is when a national moves from his own country to another. Discrimination against migrants, open or disguised, can take many forms. Reasons for migration may be the search for work or for better-paid work, or the desire to join relatives or friends, to find a more congenial climate (particularly in retirement) or to take refuge in another country for political reasons. The period of residence in another country may be long (e.g. migration for a working life) or short (for education or a limited period of work under contract) or very short (a holiday or business trip).

65 Over the past 40 years, substantial migration has taken place from countries with limited earning opportunities to countries with greater opportunities; and there has been considerable movement for political reasons. Furthermore, there has been a growing trend for elderly people to move to more congenial climates. A high proportion of the population of industrialised countries now go to another country for their holidays. As the world climbs out of the recession, economic growth is bound to be uneven between countries, and we can expect migration for work reasons to continue as in the past. Job opportunities can be created more readily in one country than in another. Access to a secure job is a critical element of economic security. In addition, there is likely to be a continued growth of newer forms of short-term visits for a variety of different reasons, of the problem of migrants stranded on arrival or suddenly deported, and of the particularly worrying problem of illegal clandestine migrants.

66 Unless special arrangements are made to prevent it, movement between countries can lead either to a loss of social security rights or to duplicated rights. The latter are wasteful of social security funds, and the former places the migrant and his or her dependants at serious risk. The consequences in terms of rights to social security may not be appreciated when the decision is taken to migrate or go abroad for other reasons.

67 Some social security rights can be exercised only within national frontiers, while new rights in another country may be acquired only by nationals and not by non-nationals, or by non-nationals only after a substantial period of residence. Thus a migrant may have accumulated very valuable rights (e.g. for pensions) which are lost and may start to acquire new rights only after a period of employment contribution or residence. For a period there may be no protection against short-term risks such as unemployment and sickness. When dependants are left behind in the country of origin, they may be denied dependency benefits and rights to health benefits because the insured person is in another country. They may no longer be eligible for family allowances or alternatively may be eligible under both national schemes. Elderly people moving abroad to a better climate or those returning home after having worked abroad may find that their pension ceases or continues to be paid at precisely the same rate in terms of money, while if they had not moved their pension would have been adjusted for changes in the cost of living. The migrant who returns home after failing to find a suitable job abroad may be treated far less favourably than if he had remained in his own country with the same work record. In all these ways, there can be a denial of social justice and unjustified discrimination between nationals and non-nationals. Moreover, lack of social security protection can be a barrier to the exercise of rights to free movement even when these rights are guaranteed by law.

68 Extensive efforts have been made to overcome these problems by bilateral and multilateral agreements with such aims as preventing discrimination between nationals and non-nationals, removing residence requirements, preserving acquired rights and rights in course of acquisition (by the technique of totalisation), transferring eligibility for benefits between national programmes, protecting the position of dependants left behind and providing rights to receive benefits in other countries. The problems are inevitably complex and vary according to different types of benefit, and often involve transfers of funds between national programmes and the use of the paying machinery in one country for the provision of benefits to which title has been earned in another. The greatest difficulties have occurred in making arrangements between two countries, in one of which rights depend solely on residence, whereas in the other they depend on contributions (paid or credited) or the employment or earnings record. There are special problems where there are marked differences in the level of benefits provided in different countries.

69 Despite the progress made, however, the situation is still far from perfect. International instruments do not always guarantee co-ordination of non-contributory benefits or minimum income provisions. Moreover, the network of international instruments now in force does not cover all major types of movements between countries. Other limiting factors continue.

70 We *recommend* that continued efforts should be made to take advantage of the framework for co-ordination of national social security arrangements outlined in the Conventions and Recommendations adopted on this subject by the International Labour Conference. We further *recommend* that international action be pursued to enlarge the network of bilateral and multilateral agreements and to achieve between them a greater measure of compatibility and co-ordination.

Harmonisation

71 Despite the differences between social security systems in various countries, arising from historical, social and economic considerations, renewed effort is needed to secure international harmonisation (if not in terms of approach, at least in terms of functions) of over-all levels of protection and of costs. This objective could be fostered by the alignment of national provisions on international standards—minimum or otherwise—embodied in the social security Conventions and Recommendations adopted by the International Labour Conference, or by regional instruments with the same purpose.

72 Since one of the main thrusts for international harmonisation has been the desirability of eliminating from international economic competition the advantages or disadvantages of different levels of social protection provided in individual States, it is desirable that the search for harmonisation should include, in particular, the question of the method of financing social security benefits.

73 We *recommend* that further efforts should be made by international action to explore the areas of social security provision in respect of which further harmonisation, particularly in the area of financing mechanisms, would be feasible; and, more generally, that adherence to existing international social security standards be recognised as a fruitful approach towards harmonisation.

Chapter 3
Developments in cash benefits

74 In the last chapter, we pointed out that social security policies had evolved with varying objectives in different countries. Some were based upon flat-rate benefits (in some cases with additions for the wife and dependent children to provide a minimum non-income-tested income as a right); others provided benefits related to previous earnings, so as to go some way towards the maintenance of customary living standards. A modest addition to benefits might be paid for a dependent wife. But within flat-rate benefit programmes a further crucial distinction has developed. On the one hand, there are those which are contribution-based in the sense that rights to benefits depend on contributions paid. On the other hand, there are provisions which cover all residents: the right to benefit depends solely on being of a certain age (leading to the right to a demogrant) or satisfying the medical criteria for being classed as a disabled person. This last type of provision is financed either from taxation or from what is in effect a hypothetical tax for social security purposes.

75 Running parallel to either type of arrangement, there is usually separate provision for occupational injury and industrial disease, which traces its origins to the right of compensation derived from the civil law established before comprehensive social security was developed. Thus those who are proved to be disabled as a result of their work, though normally employees only, obtain higher benefits than those disabled for other reasons.

76 Countries which developed an insurance-based approach were extending by law precedents developed in friendly societies, in trade unions or in occupational programmes to cover eventually the whole, or virtually the whole, of the gainfully occupied population. This method of approach carried with it the advantage that it generated its own source of revenue: the contributions of those entitled to the benefits and of employers. Thus, benefits could be provided without burdening the general taxpayer. And compared with many forms of taxation, the revenue was rela-

tively easily collected, both because of the simplicity of the calcu-
lation of contributions and because the employee had an interest
in seeing that the employer complied.

Failings in coverage

77 In social terms, however, systems of social security based
on the principle that benefits depend strictly on contributions paid or earnings covered have disadvantages. First, they exclude those who cannot earn: those physically or mentally disabled,
either from birth or before reaching working age. Second, they
exclude those who cannot get established in the labour market in
times of high unemployment and those undergoing training in the
hope of re-entering it. Moreover, rights to unemployment benefits
are often of limited duration. Third, in some countries, they
exclude part-time workers and make inadequate provision for low
earners and irregular earners. Fourth, in most countries, the self-
employed are covered only in part or not at all for occupational
injury benefits. Fifth, women who are outside the labour force,
caring for children or other dependants or simply their husbands,
earn no benefits in their own right. Their work in the home is not
recognised as work for earnings-related social security benefits, even
though their labours have enabled their husbands to prosper. The
device frequently used to provide for this last problem has been to
give married women limited rights based on their husbands' contributions, e.g. pensions if they survived their husbands. But where
women have not earned adequate rights of their own, this has
extended the dependency of married women on their husbands into
old age and denied them any rights to benefits should they become
sick or disabled while their husbands were alive.

78 Many present social security systems fail to provide for
situations of dependency which arise independently of
marriage or when marriages break up. A women with dependent
children and no paid work who cohabits with a man may acquire
no rights to benefit. Moreover, social insurance does not normally

cover the risk of separation or divorce, even though, if the ex-husband forms a new relationship, he cannot support two families on one low wage. On divorce the woman may no longer share in her husband's retirement pension and may lose the right to survivors' benefits. All rights may be transferred to a new marital partner if the ex-husband remarries. In short, many systems were originally based, and some still are based, on three key assumptions: that children were not or should not be born out of wedlock; that marriages were indissoluble; and that the normal, if not also the socially desirable, role of a woman was to be a housewife and mother without paid work, accepting total financial dependence on her husband.

79 These assumptions are no longer valid. And to some extent they never were valid. Over the past 40 years the trend in industrialised countries has been for a strikingly higher proportion of women, including married women and single women with dependent children, to take paid work. Depending on the extent of provision of day nurseries and nursery schools, and the extent of subsidisation of such provisions, women tend to return to work part-time or whole-time much earlier after the birth of a child than was generally the case in the past. Moreover, the fall in the birth rate has reduced the number of children needing to be reared. Thus, women have been earning for themselves improved rights to social security. But this does not solve all the problems. In a strict insurance system, where pensions depend on the length of working life, women lose pension rights for periods of absence from work or for only part-time work caused by responsibilities for the care of children or disabled or infirm relatives. Moreover, a break in employment normally involves a loss of seniority due to a change of employment. This is one of the many reasons why, on average, women earn less than men and thus earn title to substantially lower pensions than men.

80 On the other hand, the growth in employment opportunities for women has created situations, if still relatively rare,

where the wife earns more than the husband and where the wife
has a job and the husband is unemployed. Such situations make it
increasingly anomalous for survivors' benefits to be paid to widows
but not to widowers, which is still the practice in many countries,
though exceptions may be made where the husband is too disabled
to be able to earn.

81 But the most fundamental challenge to traditional systems
of social security is the fact that marriages are no longer
indissoluble unions between one man and one woman. Despite the
growth and importance of marriage counselling services, not only
do more and more marriages end in separation and divorce but a
growing proportion of both men and women marry more than once
in a lifetime. While the family is less often a stable and permanent
association, the family way of living in intimate domestic groups,
in which sexual mating takes place and children are reared, is still
as popular, if not more popular, than ever before. But some women
who have assumed family responsibilities do not remarry and thus
acquire no social security rights from a new husband and have
earned virtually no rights on their own account. And cohabitees
have acquired no rights to lose if the relationship ends for reasons
other than death. Moreover, the termination of any relationship in
which one party is financially dependent on the other can cause a
substantial drop in the standard of living of the dependant.

82 These new life-styles and new patterns of living pose new
problems to which social security programmes will need to
adjust. In some countries, adjustments have already begun to be
made. At first sight, flat-rate benefits which are not contributions-
based need no special adjustment, as pensions are based on current
circumstances (single or married) and not on past history. But the
problem of the definition of marriage still remains. If married
couples receive less than two single persons, there is a financial
disincentive to marry, and public opinion inevitably questions the
equity of treating two persons living together as man and wife more
favourably than persons who are legally man and wife, though this

question may not be raised where brother and sister or two persons of the same sex share a common household. A similar problem of defining a family arises when social security benefits depend on income tests, as in the provision of social assistance. Where earnings-related supplementation is by a private scheme, the same questions can arise. How, for example, should rights to a benefit for a survivor be distributed between a divorced wife, a current legal wife and the cohabitee at time of death? Should a surviving dependant of the same sex be able to claim a survivors' benefit—for instance, two sisters who live together one of whom does paid work and the other does not?

83 In formulating policy for the future, we *recommend* that policies should be based on the following principles:

1. It is a denial of a basic human right and quite unacceptable to treat women by reason of their sex less favourably than men, or men less favourably than women.

2. Persons, whether married or not, who live together should each have benefits in their own right rather than be treated as dependants, whether of their husbands or any other person; and their partners should, where necessary, pay contributions to secure them out of their incomes.

3. Where rights are derived from contribution or earning records or years of insurance, each year of rights acquired by persons who live together should be shared between that couple, with benefits paid separately so that neither is deprived of self-support, and enhanced where necessary to provide an acceptable minimum.

4. Absence from the labour force for child-rearing or for the care of the disabled or infirm should be socially recognised by allowances or benefits and, where applicable, by credits towards contributory insurance.

5. The aim should be to recognise all types of couples who are sharing income when building up rights to social security.

84 Many of these broad principles should be accepted not only in basic statutory social security programmes but also in occupational plans. We develop below the implications of these principles and how they can be applied to particular categories in practice. Detailed arrangements will, however, vary according to the historical inheritance of each country.

The principle of equal rights for men and women

85 The principle of equal rights means the abandonment of the following practices where they occur:

(a) different pension ages (it is not necessarily an advantage for women to draw their pensions earlier than men: when the pension formula is based upon years of contribution, women draw lower pensions than men for this reason);

(b) different "waiting" periods before contributions are made to an occupational plan;

(c) either higher contributions or lower benefits, based upon actuarial calculations of differences in morbidity experience or expectation of life of the two sexes;

(d) the denial of any dependency benefits to women which are paid to men;

(e) the denial of rights to survivors' benefits to men on the same terms as for women;

(f) the denial of rights to a woman cohabiting with a man which would not be denied to a man cohabiting with a woman;

(g) the denial of disablement benefits or unemployment benefits to a married woman which are available to a man or single woman; and

(h) the denial of rights of parental leave or parental allowances to men which are available to women, though there must be provisions to prevent the leave being drawn concurrently by both parents.

The extension of rights for women

86 In the long run, married women should have their own rights to social security benefits and not be treated as dependants of their husbands. Those rights should give adequate security. One way of securing this is to give credits for periods of child-rearing, for the care of disabled or infirm dependants and for registered unemployment. When a married women is not receiving credits, the husband could be required to pay contributions on her behalf. This would recognise the value to him of having a full-time housewife or an unpaid partner in his farm or business. Alternatively, half his credit might automatically be recorded in her name, and vice versa.

87 An alternative, more radical and much more costly approach is for care of this kind to be recognised as a cause for paying social security benefit. At present, most social security systems provide family allowances or child benefits towards the *maintenance* of children. Financial support for a person providing care is normally only provided indirectly where an addition for a dependent wife without paid work is added on to benefits (e.g. for sickness or unemployment). The income of a couple does, however, normally fall substantially on the birth of a child, particularly a first child, as the couple drop from two earners to one earner. Social security recognises this only by a maternity benefit which does not generally extend even for the full potential period of weaning. Similarly, the income of a couple can drop substantially if either partner abandons paid work for the care of a disabled or infirm person. In this case, two persons may have to subsist on the pension of one disabled person. The drop in income or expected income is from one earner plus pension to only one pension.

88 In many countries, home helps and other domiciliary services have been developed to help to care for disabled and infirm persons in their own homes. Inevitably, paid workers expect normal working hours. But normally there is no provision for a relative or friend living with or near the person needing care to be paid to provide it, even though they would willingly accept a benefit which was below market rates of pay for providing the service and work for much longer hours; and care by them may be much more acceptable than care by a stranger.

89 This line of reasoning leads to the development of parental allowances and allowances for the infirm and disabled as social security benefits. If parental allowances are to be neutral between the sexes, they will need to be earnings-related, so that father and mother can in turn take a period off work to care for their child while their right to return to their previous work without loss of seniority is protected. If such allowances were provided, they could lead to credit for pensions, or contributions for pensions could be paid out of them.

The sharing of rights

90 Where a couple stay together, each party should have his or her own rights, based on their joint contribution or earnings record. If the couple part, the rights of both parties should be divided equally between each party for each year they were together, subject to a provision for a minimum benefit. This might be done even if they do not part. A man or woman with two marriages before pension age would have rights derived from their own records for each year when they were single, and for half the joint rights for each year of each marriage. Thus, the rights to a survivors' pension arising from a man's contributions would be split between two or more wives, depending on the duration of the relationships. Provisions for minimum pensions would prevent pensions from being too low, or each party might be allowed (say) 70 per cent of the rights up to a maximum, because they were separated, rather than the 50 per cent they would receive if they remained together.

The definition of couples

91 The problem still remains of how to define stable relationships of couples living together (other than those who are

legally married) which should be recognised for social security purposes, e.g. men and women, brother and sister, persons of the same
sex. The aim should be to recognise *de facto* income-sharing
between a couple and not just the legal obligation to maintain
arising from a marriage contract. We recognise, however, that there
are difficult and delicate administrative problems in establishing
or securing agreement to the character of particular relationships.
But the aim should be to go as far in this direction as is practicable.
Already some countries recognise common-law wives for survivors'
benefits.

One-parent families

92 While it is possible to distribute rights for pensions and
survivors after pension age on this basis, a more difficult
problem is to provide for the one-parent family. A solution adopted
in a number of countries is to provide either higher family allowances or orphans' pensions until the children can earn their own
living, and also preferential help with day nurseries when children
are below school age. This assumes that parents can return to work
or obtain work. What if they cannot? Should they be entitled to
unemployment benefit? If parental allowances were paid, the right
to claim unemployment benefit could follow on.

93 Some countries provide benefits to widowed mothers but
not to widowed fathers or to divorced, separated or single
persons caring for children of the marriage, partnership or casual
relationship. Should the principle of widowed mothers' benefits be
extended to these other categories? Benefits to widowed mothers
were developed on the presumption that the father was always the
sole or major earner. The extension of these rights to widowed
fathers can lead, in some cases, to some widowed fathers being
financially better off after the death. Moreover, there are some,
albeit rare, cases where this can occur with existing provisions for
widowed mothers. In the future, which we postulated in Chapter
1, we expect more equal job opportunities for men and women and
more equal earnings. If this occurs, such cases will be more fre-

quent. We *recommend* that provisions for widowed mothers' benefits should become benefits available to either survivor of a partnership but should be recast to reflect the relative past earnings of the parties to the partnership.

94 Under law the putative father and the deserting or divorcing husband have an obligation to maintain, and in an increasing number of countries this obligation can fall on both parties. On the other hand, many low earners cannot support two families, so this obligation cannot provide security to both families. If, on the other hand, the rights to widowed mothers' benefit were extended to all one-parent families, this would either replace the obligation to maintain (which would have major, and in many countries unacceptable, implications—including the encouragement of fictitious desertion) or it would operate on top of social security benefits. In this case, divorced and separated wives with children would be better off than widowed mothers. This could be avoided if social security schemes paid the benefit and recovered what could be recovered from the person with the legal obligation.

Survivors under pension age without dependent children

95 In most countries, either widows or survivors are provided with temporary assistance, either as a benefit for a limited period or as a lump sum (a fixed amount or a sum calculated in proportion to the final income of the deceased). As above, we *recommend* that such provisions should be recast to reflect the relative past earnings of the two parties, to prevent financial compensation for a loss which has not occurred. But where such assistance is necessary, we believe that the period should be sufficiently long to allow for readjustment. We *recommend* that a benefit should be paid for a sufficient time to enable the survivor to reorganise his or her life, to take vocational training and to look for paid work.

96 But the question arises of survival from what—the death of the partner or the termination of the relationship with a partner? Should a deserted wife or husband have the same rights to a short-term pension as a widow? Should it be restricted to persons not in full-time work at the time the desertion took place? Would such a provision encourage fictitious desertion? These are some of the difficult questions which social security programmes will be forced to answer in the coming years. Some type of transitional benefit might be paid, as recommended in paragraph 95 above, though opportunities for training may be even more important (see paragraph 99).

The unemployed

97 Traditionally, the main social security provision for the unemployed has been seen as a system to protect workers against income loss during short periods of unemployment rather than during long-term unemployment. This was to protect the funds from the type of recession involving substantial long-term unemployment, as at present. But this is in conflict with the principles of social security which we enunciated in the last chapter. Moreover, provision has been hedged around with criteria of labour market attachment and disqualification when unemployment is due to family or personal causes or dissatisfaction with the job. Part-time work is sometimes excluded. On the other hand, the work status of employees has been protected by the requirement of referral to suitable work.

98 Arrangements of this kind do not provide for problems which occur particularly among women. Indeed, they often were deliberately designed to offer protection against "abuse" by married women—claims that jobs were being sought which might have been refused if they were offered. This was one purpose of the criterion of labour market attachment. The arrangements deliberately excluded part-time work, which is all that many women can offer while bringing up a family. Finally, no provision was made for women to be retrained after bringing up their family or after divorce or separation.

__99__ We *recommend* that there should be much more extensive provision of training and retraining allowances, not only for women re-entering the labour force but also for workers or others with redundant skills or disability. After these allowances, unemployment benefits should be payable, possibly on the basis of contributions paid during the training or retraining period. We see the offer of training as a way of overcoming the problem of labour force attachment for persons re-entering the labour force after shouldering family responsibilities. The provision of parental and other allowances for those providing care can overcome the problem of persons unable to take paid work for family reasons.

__100__ We believe that part-time work should be covered by unemployment insurance. As regards unemployment in general, we believe that opportunities for retraining should be offered when people become unemployed. Where unemployment benefits are paid, they should be of unlimited duration, subject to the removal, after a period, of the "suitable work" constraint and to the possibility of a reduction in the level of benefits where these are high in relation to potential earnings. A minority of us take the view that unemployment benefits should not be of unlimited duration and that further provision should be made by social assistance.

__101__ To avoid the individual frustrations and ebbing self-confidence that produce harmful effects upon the long-term unemployed, and also as a matter of economic wisdom, we *recommend* that countries should explore the possibility of, and endeavour to implement, public employment programmes which will enable these people to retain their work skills and to achieve something for themselves and for the community.

The disabled

__102__ Where there are contribution-based rights to social security, the disabled are generally divided into three categories: those disabled as a result of work (or war), who obtain a relatively generous level of compensation; those disabled not from these causes but who are covered by social security and who receive more modest benefits; and those who are not covered by social security, particularly housewives and those with disabilities arising before working age, who generally receive help only from social assistance. Some countries have, however, introduced non-contributory benefits for the last group, but at a less generous level than those provided by social insurance so as to protect the principle of insurance: that only those who have contributed receive full benefits. Even in countries where the main social security programme is not insurance-based, provision for occupational injury and disease is often based on insurance and leads to higher benefits. In some countries, private insurance companies are used for occupational risks.

103 Three reasons are sometimes advanced in favour of a separate and more generous programme covering occupational injury and disease. The first is that the separate insurance of companies or occupations encourages employers to promote health and safety. The second is the greater risks associated with particular types of work. The third is that employees deserve more from their employers because they have been injured while acting under orders. However, these are implausible arguments, we think, when they are proffered as justification for such discrimination. A tax could be levied on firms according to their safety record, and the yield paid into the general pool to finance all social security benefits. Penalising bad risks need not be associated with better benefits. As regards the second argument, it can be claimed that it establishes a case for higher wages by way of danger money—but surely not for higher levels of compensation than others receive for the same disability. As regards the third argument, it is hard to see, negligence aside, why higher compensation should be paid because of the fact that some workers might suffer injuries while accepting normal directions. Nevertheless, it is argued that public opinion expects those injured at work or in war to be especially favoured when they become victims as a result of service which benefits the community as a whole. But whether public opinion has been formed simply by long historical experience is less easily established.

104 The arguments against "occupational preference" are the following. First, the line defining occupations as service to the community is not easily defended. The self-employed (including the bulk of doctors in many countries) are generally excluded. When, for example, self-employed farmers are included, it is not possible in practice to make a clear distinction between occupational injury and injury in the home. Also generally excluded are people doing voluntary work or training for occupations, however hazardous. So are housewives, including mothers, working in the home. Second, the line which has to be drawn between injuries and diseases that are proved to be of occupational origin and those that are not (though the working situation may have contributed to them) is thin, contentious and hard for the public, particularly the disabled public, to understand. Third is the cost to individuals and to society of legal disputes about this line and, where private insurance is involved, the high legal and administrative costs built into the premiums. Fourth, the claim for occupational preference disregards the many dangerous hazards which affect everyone outside the working day. The working environment is not wholly distinct from the environment in which people spend the rest of their lives. For all these reasons, there is growing support for the view that it is the degree of disability and the losses caused by it which should lead to different levels of benefit rather than the cause—an argument strongly pressed by organisations representing disabled people, the majority of whom were not disabled from their work.

105 A unified system of disability benefits which treats all disabled people on similar principles, with a common administration and system of financing, would not necessarily give precisely the same level of benefit to all those with the same disability. Those who have suffered a loss of earnings (partial or total) as a result of their disability can be given an element of benefit which takes account of this loss. But other provisions can be based on the degree of disability rather than on the cause of disability. For example, allowances can be given according to the extent of need for attendance. Those who cannot use public transport can be given an allowance to enable them to use other, more expensive forms of transport, such as taxis or a family car. Other allowances can be provided to take account of any further extra costs (e.g. clothing) resulting from being a disabled person.

106 Apart from the vested interests of lawyers and insurance companies, where they are involved, a further large obstacle to achieving a unified system is the cost of upgrading all benefits for disabled people to the level of those received under the "occupational preference". While a social insurance fund can look to higher contributions to pay for the increase, benefits for those not covered by insurance will need to be financed by the taxpayer. Alternatively, all disability benefits can be financed wholly by taxation, as is the practice for family allowances in a substantial number of countries, but this is not likely to be popular in countries where the tax-resistance lobby is powerful.

107 In some countries, the administrative problems of merging different agencies, agreeing on a common definition of disability and establishing a common financing system and the political problems of removing experience-rating will be formidable. For all these reasons, we do not expect progress to be made quickly in every country towards a unified system of disability benefits. But the majority of us *recommend* that it is in this direction that policy should move in stages, as resources permit and as public opinion comes to accept the justice of the case. It is not an impossible target for all industrialised countries by the year 2000.

108 Some members would qualify this recommendation. Even under a unified programme there should still be provisions for contributions from employers, whether experience-rated or not,

to cover a differential benefit for workers injured in the course of
their employment. The aim would be to provide them with extra
compensation, beyond reimbursement for health care expenses and
replacement of lost income, in recognition of the damages they
have suffered owing to the negligence of, or inadequate precautions
taken by, their employers.

Pension age

109 We have argued above that it is not acceptable for men
and women to receive pensions at different ages. Where
such differences exist, the question posed is whether the pension
age for women should be steadily raised step by step to that of
men, whether the pension age for men should be lowered to that
of women, or whether an equal pension age should be established
somewhere between the present two ages.

110 By pension age we mean the age at which pension can first
be drawn. We believe it to be socially undesirable to insist
on retirement as a condition for drawing pension. Older people
should not be denied the right to work, or threatened with the loss
of pension rights if they choose to do so. Nor should people be
forced to start drawing their pension at the earliest age at which
they are entitled to it. If they wish to postpone drawing their pension, they should be entitled to a higher pension at the time at
which they choose to claim it. Pension age should not be confused
with the age of retirement.

111 With the present high level of unemployment heavily concentrated on young people seeking to enter the labour force,
it is argued that the industrialised countries should be moving
towards lower pension ages. Older workers should be encouraged
to retire by the offer of pensions at a lower age, so that their jobs
can be taken by young people: each day out of work is a particularly damaging economic and social experience for the young.
Where programmes of early retirement have been introduced, however, it has been found that substantially fewer new workers are

taken on than are retired, as employers take the opportunity to introduce new work processes which need less labour. They have, in fact, been tolerating considerable overmanning and retaining redundant technology to avoid dismissing older workers. Thus early retirement programmes enable them to achieve higher levels of labour productivity. Nevertheless, some still argue for lower pension ages, on the grounds that even a small increase in job opportunities for young workers would justify the cost of lowering the pension age.

112 There are others who argue that, as pensions are the largest element in the cost of social security, the only way in which the cost can be prevented from becoming an impossible burden on the economy is by raising the pension age. As the expectation of life has been increasing and standards of health have been improving, people can work longer before the availability of pensions gives them the option to retire. Against this it is argued that, if one looks beneath the averages, one finds a substantial proportion of people who are not fit to continue to work even up to existing pension ages. Moreover, a considerable proportion still die before drawing their pension. Thus a higher pension age would be particularly unjust to unskilled manual workers, who pay disproportionately for pensions which they do not live long enough to claim.

113 As mentioned in Chapter 1, our report is based on the relatively optimistic view that, in the longer run, jobs and jobseekers will achieve a better balance. Thus we consider it wrong in principle to take the fundamental and very costly step of lowering the pension age to meet the needs of what, in the light of history, will come to be seen as a temporary situation. We give higher pensions a greater financial priority than reducing the age for claiming them.

114 Thus, if in particular countries older workers are to be induced to leave the labour force in the hope that jobs will be found for young workers, any such arrangements should be distinct from the general provision for pensions. Offers can be made to firms to pay a special high level of unemployment or redundancy benefit to older workers whom they retire, on condition that each early retirement leads to a job for a younger worker. Alternatively, special offers can be made once and for all to older workers in industries most likely to replace early retired workers. Any such programmes should be seen to be temporary and reversible rather than permanent and selective, and to be conditional rather than general. In our view, old-age insurance is the wrong instrument to use for attempts to alleviate the current economic crisis.

115 The design of pension programmes, both statutory and non-statutory, should be based on social rather than economic considerations, though to a certain extent both point in the same direction. The aim should be to give each individual the maximum choice and flexibility about how much paid work is done at any age, according to health and personal preference. There is evidence that compulsory and total retirement at a fixed age can have traumatic psychological effects on some individuals. For those without many outside interests and social life, dismissal from the social contacts of the workplace, the abandonment of the routine of working life and the loss of meaningful activity can result in feelings of isolation and rejection and even lead to early death. Meaningful activity is the best protection against the ageing process, and some find it in work. Thus compulsory retirement practices should be abandoned. We *recommend* that the employer should be required to prove that a worker is no longer able to do any work which he can offer before he can impose retirement. This means that employers should be required to accept the responsibility of retraining older workers for work suited to their changing capacities.

116 No less important are opportunities to make a gradual transition between work and retirement. We *recommend* that employees and the self-employed should be given the right to reduce their weekly working time, with a corresponding reduction in earnings, as they get older. Parallel to this, pension plans for the aged should be made more flexible, so that beneficiaries can draw only part of their pension rights during this period of transition. This could be of special benefit to women (e.g. grandparents who care for their grandchildren). The amount of these rights which each individual chooses to draw in a particular year, subject to a maximum, should be left to the individual to decide. Any rights not drawn in any one year should be allowed to accumulate, thus increasing pension rights for later years. Social security administrators must recognise that social security benefits are designed for people, and bureaucratic procedures must be adjusted to accommodate individual choice.

117 We do not, however, believe that the annual maximum right to pension should necessarily be the same for each year. There is a strong case for the pension being higher when elderly people become infirm and need the assistance of others. Moreover, where part of the pension comes from a programme where the pension is not fully indexed, the case for this becomes even stronger. One way to make such a provision is to pay an allowance based on evidence of infirmity. An alternative is to increase the pension from age 75 or 80. The extent of the bonus or extra allowance will depend on the extent to which free or subsidised services, such as domestic help or meals-on-wheels, are available. But we see advantage in putting elderly people in a position to pay in part for services, as it widens their range of choice and reduces feelings of dependence.

Chapter 4

Developments in services

Prevention and rehabilitation

118 We are in no doubt that the development of services for prevention and rehabilitation should receive the highest priority in social security policy for the period up to the year 2000 and beyond. Up to the present, social security has tended to concentrate on providing access to what are mainly curative health services and on providing cash in defined contingencies. While efforts have been made to prevent contingencies from arising and to reduce the frequency of their occurrence in a number of countries, progress has so far been uneven, both within and between countries. Prevention needs to permeate virtually all departments of government, the actions of employers and employees, the activities of voluntary bodies and, most important of all, the actions of individuals and families.

119 The prevention of risks is itself an addition to personal and collective security. Some preventive actions (for example, accident prevention) will produce immediate savings in cash benefits and health care costs. Some actions may postpone costs: they may even add to long-term costs if people draw their pensions longer and live long enough to face mental and physical infirmity. We do not, however, believe that assessments of the costs and benefits of particular preventive measures should be the criteria for guiding policies in this area or for establishing priorities. The criterion should be the contribution which preventive action can make to the quality of life—particularly the quality of life of the less privileged.

120 One of the most important risks is that of redundancy. With the rapid changes in skill requirements for employment, the risks may well be still greater in the future than they have been in the past. Retraining and continuing education are ways of reducing these risks. In addition, governmental action may be needed to encourage the generation of new jobs. Moreover, it may be cheaper (at least in the short term) to maintain jobs by subsidy than to pay out unemployment benefits. The prevention of unemployment by a whole variety of measures should be a high priority for social security policy in the widest sense.

121 By rehabilitation we mean comprehensive and inter-related services dedicated to the total welfare of disabled or socially disadvantaged persons. For children, the emphasis will be on developmental, educational and social activities: for adults, it will be on the restoration of the capacity for work, whether paid or unpaid, including retraining for a new occupation. Where in the case of the aged, the severely injured or those with progressive chronic illness work will not be feasible, the objective will be to prevent further deterioration and to maintain the highest possible standards of health, self-care and social effectiveness. The services needed include assessment, physical restoration, the provision of aids and appliances and training in their use, personal and vocational counselling, alterations in the home to meet the needs of the disabled, education and vocational training, job placement and follow-up of progress in the job. The ultimate aim is to sustain and integrate the disabled in life at work or in school, in the home and in the community.

122 We list in the next paragraph some of the key areas for action. This list does not pretend to be exhaustive. Moreover, if prevention is given the emphasis we believe it justifies, this must be carried through into priorities for research in the biological sciences and, no less important, in the social sciences. The more we understand causes, the more potential fields for preventive action will be identified. But research must progress beyond diagnosis into action. We need to know much more about how to apply the knowledge we already have. For example, to know in what way people ought to change their behaviour is not enough. We need to understand the obstacles to change, how best they can be overcome, and how individuals and families can be motivated to want to change their own behaviour.

123 Thus the list below is given to illustrate the breadth of action which is encompassed and the extent to which policies are inter-related.

1. *Health policy.* The causes of sickness and death can be found in human biology, in the social and economic environment, in life-style and, to a lesser extent, in failings in the health care system. The aims include:

   (a) improving the social and economic environment by preventing exposure to hazardous substances, improving housing, combating poverty, unemployment and violence, and promoting safer facilities for travel, safer homes and a safer working environment;

   (b) encouraging healthier life-styles by cutting out cigarette smoking, the abuse of drugs and alcohol, obesity and unhealthy eating habits and by promoting exercise, the use of seat-belts, safer driving and safer working practices. They may involve, for example, legal regulation, tax policy and the provision of facilities for sport, as well as health education and community action;

   (c) providing occupational health services to adjust jobs to the health of workers;

   (d) providing medical rehabilitation, aids and adaptations for the disabled, screening which is cost-effective, ante- and post-natal care, food supplementation for pregnant mothers and young children, immunisation services and regular assessment of the health of young children; and

   (e) preventing the birth of damaged children.

2. *Family and population policy.* Support for families under strain, emergency child care in crisis situations, marriage, family and pregnancy counselling, day care, continuing education for young mothers, family planning, birth control information, home helps, home nursing and day hospitals and facilities for the temporary care of disabled and infirm family members while the person providing care goes on holiday.

3. *Employment policy.* Adequate placement services, vocational
   guidance, training and retraining (particularly for disabled
   workers, older workers with redundant skills and women re-
   entering the labour force after child-rearing or on divorce or
   widowhood), continuing education, subsidies for relocation, job
   creation and subsidy, the promotion of community service
   schemes, the control of immigration.

4. *Social welfare policies.* Counselling for the bereaved and separated, crisis intervention services, integration services, services
   to support one-parent families and to postpone the ageing process by occupation, activity and social contact and a whole range
   of services to promote care in people's own homes and so in the
   community; and also to limit the loss of autonomy involved
   when institutional care of the aged and disabled cannot be
   avoided.

124 Preventive policy will need to be closely co-ordinated and
priorities will need to be established, observed and moni-
tored between different fields of action to secure the most efficient
use of all resources. The criterion should be to maximise the quality
of life. We are well aware that this concept is not value-free and
will be defined and interpreted in different ways according to the
cultural traditions of different nations, communities and ethnic
groups.

125 We discuss below this problem of priorities between and
within two main groups of services: the health services and
the social services, in which we include family and employment
policy as well as social welfare. However, we regard this division
as somewhat artificial. It is nevertheless a distinction found in
virtually all countries. The aim in the future should be to secure
greater co-ordination between services and between professionals
with different skills and training.

Health services

126 Over the past 40 years, there has been an unprecedented development in medical technology. While some developments (for example, in pharmaceuticals) have widespread applications, some of the most costly developments have benefited relatively small groups of patients with particular conditions. The ratio between what can usefully be spent on a particular patient in a short period and his earnings for that period has increased enormously. For this reason, protection against the costs of health care, whether through a service model or through a pure insurance model, has never been more needed.

127 While health care costs amounted to around 4 per cent of gross domestic product in most industrialised countries in the early 1950s, by the early 1980s health care costs are approaching 10 per cent of gross domestic product in several countries. On the other hand, in those countries where the central oversight of expenditures has been possible by providing health care against predetermined budgets, governments have succeeded in securing a much more moderate growth of health care costs in relation to national resources. If the predetermined budget figure is exceeded in a particular year, the local organisation can be assisted from outside to avoid the same planning or administrative mistakes in future.

128 The trend towards higher health care costs is due to the following reasons, not all of which operate in every country:

(a) the expansion of medical technology mentioned above;
(b) the increased coverage of health insurance, both in the proportion of the population and in the range of benefits;
(c) the ageing of the population;
(d) the greater survival rate of seriously disabled persons;
(e) higher relative pay for nurses and ancillary staff, due to increased unionisation and equal pay for women;

(f) the relative price effect, due to the labour intensiveness of the
health sector;

(g) the easing or removal of supply constraints, in particular:

  (i) increases in the ratio of doctors per 1,000 population: this
  is of major importance because it is doctors who authorise
  the use of the main health resources such as consultations,
  examinations, drugs, diagnostic tests and hospital care; and

  (ii) increases in the ratio of general hospital beds per 1,000
  population and/or the rebuilding of much of the general
  hospital stock;

(h) incentives operating on doctors, dentists and hospitals to provide more health care;

(i) the more sophisticated expectations of the public;

(j) lack of competition in pricing health care services; and

(k) insufficient application of modern organisational techniques in
the health service delivery system, i.e. limited use of group
clinics with central administrative and support services and
specialisations in diagnostics and treatment.

129 Some of these trends are bound to continue up to the year
2000 and beyond—the increasing proportion of the elderly
in the population, the relative price effect within the real growth
of national economies, and further developments in medical technology. In some countries, moreover, there is room for a further
expansion of health insurance. It would be undesirable to limit
medical progress or to restrict access to the benefits of medical
technology which can *demonstrably* improve the quality of life. As
our societies become richer, it is in this area that we are convinced
that people want to see more money spent—particularly on improvements in the quality of care given to the aged and to the dying
as well as in the life prospects of children.

130 While the improvements in the quality of life of many
groups of patients with particular conditions have been

enormous over the past 30 years, the extent of improvement of health in general should not be exaggerated, for the following reasons:

1. While both infant and maternal mortality have fallen sharply, the vast increase in health spending has not led to a general acceleration in the decline in the mortality rates compared with the previous 30 years.
2. Spending more on curative services does not necessarily bring better health.
3. Despite the increased coverage of social security, there has been no narrowing in the relative gaps in health status between socio-economic groups in those countries which have attempted to measure these differences.

131 From this analysis we draw five conclusions which should guide priorities over the years ahead:

1. As mentioned above, the prevention of ill health, in its widest sense, has been relatively neglected compared with the vast investment in curative medicine. While in the more liberal systems of providing health care doctors are in a position to authorise virtually any use of resources which may conceivably help in the cure of their patients and are subject to financial incentives to do so, expenditure on preventive measures is subject to tight budget limits, and is inadequately promoted and co-ordinated within government. Within many health insurance systems, only narrowly defined preventive acts are rewarded, and preventive advice and education of the patient leads to no extra reward at all.
2. While there are powerful financial and professional incentives to promote medical activity which might possibly improve the quality of life and postpone death, social welfare action which can contribute to precisely the same objectives is budget-limited, underfinanced and, in some countries, stigmatising and subject to financing barriers which are not applied for medically authorised care.

3. Within many health care systems, resources are not used in a cost-effective way. For example:

   (a) costly general hospital beds are used to care for patients who could be looked after as effectively in less costly ways, such as nursing homes, outpatient diagnosis, day hospitals, day surgery and care at home with the support of domiciliary services;

   (b) mentally ill and mentally retarded patients are treated in costly specialised hospitals when they could be cared for in hostels or in the community with the support of appropriate home care services;

   (c) costly equipment is underutilised, or used where cheaper alternatives could be no less effective;

   (d) some surgical and other procedures are used unnecessarily;

   (e) drugs are excessively used and may cost far more than in neighbouring countries;

   (f) specialists provide services which could be effectively provided by general practitioners;

   (g) general practitioners or specialists provide services which could be effectively provided by nurses and paramedicals;

   (h) diagnostic tests are used unselectively; and

   (i) health resources are unevenly distributed between poor and rich areas of the country and between the inner cities and the prosperous growing suburbs.

   Yet it has been increasingly recognised that cost can no longer be regarded as a marginal issue in medical practice. It has now become an essential aspect of clinical practice.

4. There is an urgent need to re-examine the professional education of health and medical personnel to emphasise: the importance of prevention of illness; the importance of a holistic approach to the health of the individual and family; the economics of health problems; the responsibility of the individual and the community for maintaining and preserving good physical and

mental health; and the right of individuals to be informed
of the alternatives to treatment recommended by health professionals.

5. Most health care systems have been designed by providers for
the provided without any consultation or involvement of local
people. Only for a narrow range of conditions does the health
care system seek out those who ought to be receiving care. And
in some systems it would be regarded as unfair market competition to do so. Generally, people are assumed to know when
they ought to seek care. When care is sought, it is often in a relationship of subordination and coercion of the patient rather than
in a co-operative counsellor relationship of equals. This has
tended to deprive people of a sense of responsibility for their
own health and encourages them to regard the health care
system as an authoritarian repair shop for their body. The relationships established differ, however, between social classes. It
is partly due to these features that the social groups with the
greatest need use it less than their health warrants.

132 We *recommend* that priorities should be increasingly
asserted over the coming years to achieve the most cost-
effective use of health services, to change the balance between curative action and preventive action and between medically authorised
action and socially authorised action and to enable people to play
a greater role in decision-making about their own health and social
care. The challenge for the rest of this century is how to go beyond
the removal of money barriers to the removal of barriers of class,
knowledge and culture and how to make use correspond to need.

133 Different countries will no doubt find different ways of
increasing the cost effectiveness of the use of health
resources. Already more and more countries are recognising that
they have an excess of general hospital beds, and that when such
beds are provided they tend to be used inappropriately. Thus, different systems of planning new developments on a regional or

national basis have been developed. But it is also increasingly
recognised in many countries that limiting new developments is
not enough. Many general hospital beds already provided need to
be closed or transferred to other uses. Such changes tend to be
heavily resisted both by local populations and by hospital staffs.
At the same time, alternative forms of care which are less costly
need to be developed.

134 Similarly, more and more countries have come to recognise
that they have trained too many doctors, that still more
are under training, that within medicine too many doctors are
obtaining specialist qualifications and that market forces fail to
secure an acceptable distribution of medical manpower.

135 The type of changes which this analysis implies will require
the modification of rights long established in some
countries and long abolished or never granted in others. These
include:

(a) the right of any qualified student to study medicine;

(b) the right to be trained in any speciality of choice;

(c) the right of doctors to establish themselves in social-security-
paid practice wherever they choose;

(d) the right for *any* doctor to decide that a patient should be
admitted to or discharged from hospital;

(e) the right of medical associations or individual doctors to choose
their system of payment and to establish the relative fees which
will be paid wholly or partly by social security;

(f) the right of the patient to visit as many doctors as the *patient*
chooses during the course of an episode of illness and for all
these services to be covered by social security; and

(g) the right of the *patient* to choose into which hospital he or she
will be admitted with the full cost covered by social security.

136 In some countries, there is discussion of ways by which the
consumer can be equipped to make choices between dif-

ferent types of insurance policy at different prices under social
security, so that the cost consciousness of the consumer will force
providers to be more cost conscious. Such policies, if they are successful, are intended to drive some hospitals into bankruptcy and
closure and to create unemployed and underemployed doctors. In
other countries, it is hoped that teaching health economics to doctors and making clear both to them and to their patients the costs
which are being generated will go some way to encouraging cost
effectiveness. Other countries are aiming to achieve similar results
by regulations and planning. Countries with budget-based systems
of health care are in a stronger position to establish priorities, close
facilities which are no longer needed, to plan their health manpower training policies to achieve a desired balance of different
categories of manpower working in their health services, and to
contain their health care costs within planned budget limits.

137 In more and more countries, greater use is being made of
cost sharing or charges, in order to raise revenue, to avoid
unnecessary use and, partly, to use the cost consciousness of the
patient as a signal to the provider. Some systems of cost sharing
can have perverse results. If charges are made for out-of-hospital
care while care in hospital is without charge, more care may be
provided in the most costly way. Cost sharing, for example on consultations or drugs, may lead to the low income groups making
fewer demands, so that providers generate more services for the
higher income groups to maintain their incomes. In general, we do
not believe that cost sharing is an ideal way of achieving the
desired results in the long term. In so far as the utilisation of the
lowest income group is influenced most, it is in this income group
that there is the largest gap between use and need. If it becomes
substantial, it amounts to "de-insurance": it defeats the whole purpose of social security.

138 *We are convinced that countries which have not done so will
need to find ways of making their health care systems more
cost effective.* Decisions will need to be taken long before the year

2000 about the way in which this should be done. In some
countries, established traditions and freedoms will have to be
modified if the growth of costs is to be moderated and new priorities are to be established. This is inevitable. The aim should be
to use the level of staff and the level of scientific and administrative technology appropriate to the particular task.

139 In this context we commend the principles established at
the international conference on primary health care that
was held at Alma-Ata in 1978 under the joint sponsorship of the
World Health Organisation and the United Nations Childrens'
Fund.[1] Those principles were endorsed by all highly industrialised
countries at the World Health Assembly in 1980. *The key to
securing the use of appropriate technology is a system of primary
health care which:*

(a) is accessible and acceptable to *all* users;

(b) integrates preventive and curative care;

(c) uses multidisciplinary teams of doctors and other workers;

(d) involves continuity of care and organised referral to secondary
care; and

(e) includes the participation of the population served.

The social services

140 The social services will need to have a greater role over the
next 20 years, for the following reasons:

(a) the ageing of the population and particularly the growth in proportion of elderly;

(b) the trend for women to live longer than men, so that more and
more women survive their husbands;

(c) the increasing trend for adult children to find jobs which are
geographically distant from the homes of their parents and, in
some countries, for people to change their homes after retirement;

(d) the increase in the proportion of women with paid work;

(e) the need for a wider development of family and marriage counselling with the aim of preventing marriage break-up where this
is possible;

(f) the possible further growth in the number of single-parent
families, owing to the greater incidence of break-up of marriages;

(g) the need for concerted efforts to develop training and retraining
in view of the likelihood of an even more rapid need for
changes in skills, in response to technological developments
both in industry and in services;

(h) the relative underdevelopment of social services in most
countries today, as noted above;

(i) the low probability of achieving full employment and therefore
a continuing pool of unemployed persons;

(j) the continuing upward trend in prices and therefore the depreciation in the value of personal savings; and

(k) the increased isolation of individuals owing to family shrinkage
and the impersonality of urban expansion.

141 As the traditional family structure is in a position to provide less of the support needed to vulnerable groups, the
gaps will need to be filled by social services working in partnership
with family members, neighbours, volunteers and non-profit organisations. In the past, the provision of social service help was
regarded as a sign of incompetence or personal failure. It is now
accepted that there are common needs in all income groups and
that social service help may be required to meet them. As working
hours are reduced and as more people choose to retire early, more
emphasis will need to be placed on recreation, leisure and cultural
activities, and not solely for the aged and disabled. Moreover, as
more and more specialised facilities develop and more social rights
are provided, people need more information and advice on what
is available: some may need advocates to help them to assert their
rights.

142 Just as health services may prevent, cure, rehabilitate or simply provide care, so social services can perform four functions in parallel with or apart from health services. They can *prevent* conditions that cause disadvantage or disability. They can *protect* those whose safety or well-being is at risk, such as the aged, the disabled, battered wives, or children lacking suitable parental care. They can *rehabilitate* those who have withdrawn from normal social life, such as alcoholics, drug addicts, the bereaved and divorced, the aged, the disabled, the mentally ill, ex-inmates of penal institutions, immigrants and members of ethnic minorities. Finally, they can help certain people and communities *to develop their potential,* including those with limited employability, the mentally retarded, families overwhelmed with debt and other problems, and communities in need of the help of social animators, advocates and organisers of structures for citizen participation. A service can perform more than one function for an individual, family or community.

143 No less than health services, they can make a major contribution to the quality of life of individuals and families. The provision of domestic help and the mobilisation of the support of friends, neighbours and other agencies may enable aged people to continue to live in the community. Aids and adaptations to the home may enable disabled people not only to continue to live in their own homes but also to go out and participate in community life. Children with a grossly unsatisfactory home situation may be enabled to make a new life with foster parents or be adopted by a new family. A family may be overshadowed by chronic debt or poverty, or threatened with eviction, because of lack of information or the skills to badger agencies into providing its full entitlements to social security benefits. Yet hardly anywhere are social service agencies in a position to meet anything like all the needs which, in their professional opinion, would contribute to the quality of life.

144 In this respect, they are in a contrasting position to the health services in the same country. While, in more and

more countries, it is recognised that all citizens should have the
right to health care, in many countries, eligibility to social services
is at present limited to those who need social assistance or some
other mechanism for income-tested financial support. Moreover,
often the agency that provides cash also provides services, and the
provision of cash may be made conditional on (or be believed to
be conditional on) the acceptance of specific services, such as
budget counselling. There must be an automatic right to health
care, but that right is essentially a right of access to the services;
beyond that automatic right of access, what is actually provided
must depend on professional assessment. Similarly, everyone may
need information from the social services and advice and help with
situations of crisis. The need for certain types of services, such as
day care, home help or mobile aids, should be based on professional assessment. The provision of social services should not be
restricted to those receiving social assistance or be conditional upon
it. Ideally, access to social services should not be denied solely on
financial grounds, for example, to people who are just above some
income limit, or to people who cannot pay the full user charge for
a needed service.

145 The following two principles should be applied in the social
services:

1. All income groups should be able to seek help from the social
   services: their use by higher income groups removes the stigma
   of separate services provided exclusively for poor people.
2. People should be coerced, or believe they may be coerced, into
   using social services by the threat of withdrawal of cash assistance.

146 In many countries, social service agencies are fragmented
by target group, social problems, religious affiliation or
source of funds. This leads to duplicated effort and multiple contacts for a family with multiple types of need for services. Hence
some countries have reorganised local services to provide a com-

prehensive approach, so that users receive continuity of care and
so that all their needs can be co-ordinated through the same agency,
though referrals may be made for more specialised help. Just as the
central importance of the general practitioner has become increasingly recognised as the pivot in the health care system, so there are
moves to establish what are, in effect, primary social care centres
to co-ordinate the variety of specialised social agencies and to point
users in the direction of those services most suited to their needs.
This development is in no way intended to replace voluntary and
private agencies and voluntary workers, but rather to mobilise more
voluntary help and to encourage community participation and community action.

147 We *recommend* that there should be a major development
of social services in the period up to the year 2000. We
make this recommendation for three reasons:
1. Social needs are bound to increase, for the reasons given above.
2. The development of social services is essential to securing the
   cost-effective use of health services.
3. Social services can contribute to the quality of life no less than
   health services.

148 Second, we *recommend* that there should be a right of
access to social services as they are developed and in a
practical sense become available, parallel to the right of *access* to
health services, without prohibitive financial barriers.

149 Third, we *recommend* that social services should be co-
ordinated locally to provide comprehensive help and support and continuity of care to families and individuals. This should
be a responsibility of government in consultation with interested
groups.

150 Fourth, we *recommend* that mechanisms should be established to secure community and non-profit agency partici-

pation in the planning and running of local health and social welfare services.

Note

[1] World Health Organisation: *Primary health care,* Report of the International Conference on Primary Health Care, Alma-Ata, USSR, 6-12 September 1978, jointly sponsored by the World Health Organisation and the United Nations Children's Fund (Geneva, 1978).

Chapter 5

Relations with the public

151 As mentioned in Chapter 1, social security now occupies a major place in national economies. The cost of social security can amount to up to a third of national income in some cases. It has thus become a major structural element in our societies. It should therefore be seen as a unified whole, not as an aggregate of separate benefits to which citizens are entitled. The term "welfare state" is often used rather than "social security" to describe the underlying philosophy and give it a unity in public discussion.

Public attitudes

152 Yet people have contradictory attitudes towards it. On the one hand, they protest that it is too costly; on the other hand, it is readily used without consideration of cost. Indeed, there is little real understanding of why it costs what it does. People take it for granted and yet resent paying for it. Part of the reason is that the really major costs go on particular groups with whom the bulk of people do not readily identify. Above all else, social security is a compact between generations. People pay when young to be looked after when they become old. Tomorrow's young will in turn pay for tomorrow's old. Yet old age seems remote to the young and even the middle-aged, and the cost of the intensive health and social care which may need to be given to those who are severely ill, and particularly those in the last years of life, is not appreciated. People receiving most from social security are not visible on the streets and in the shops. And even they do not know the cost of what they receive.

153 Only in recent years has the bulk of the working population come to appreciate that unemployment could happen to them. Yet a section of the population is still reluctant to see money go to people without work. There is a suspicion that some unemployed people could get a job if they really wanted to, that some are scroungers living on the backs of other people. In particular, those with tough manual jobs resent people getting money without

working for it. Whatever the facts, there is a suspicion that the
administration of social security is too lax and that the unemployed
have a soft life, or more generous benefits than is in fact the case.
And there are further suspicions that large numbers of people are
receiving benefits while earning, particularly in the "black" or
underground economy. The extent of this problem of fraud tends
to be fanned by the popular press out of all proportion, reflecting
the prejudices of readers. The result is extremely damaging for
popular support and willingness to subscribe to social security.

154 Social security has grown to a vast size without developing
an adequate public information and public education service commensurate with its magnitude. While large firms spend
lavishly to inform the public about their activities and to build up
their image, social security spends relatively little. Moreover, the
message it has to convey is far more complex. One reason for this
failure in public relations is the fragmentary structure which charac-
terises social security in so many countries. Even where social
security is largely unified under government, the cheeseparing attitudes of custodians of public money come into play. Money can
be saved by printing forms on low quality paper and cramming too
many questions on a page. Leaflets can be packed with close type.
And general image advertising may be ruled out as being politically
contentious—as appearing to promote the particular government
of the day. When public co-operation is needed with some administrative procedure, the cheapest way of securing it is found. The
effort is concentrated on what the public is expected to do rather
than why they need to do it, or on the institution of social security
which is giving daily and indispensable service to the public.

Education

155 Thus social security has grown to a vast size in a fog of
public ignorance about it. Though there are some new
developments, in most countries there is no systematic education

about the spending of up to a third of national income in primary schools or even in secondary schools. Children can leave school with only the haziest idea about how up to a third of the value of their work will be spent. Nor is study of social security firmly based in university courses. Often it is scattered around as part of the faculties of law or given some brief attention in courses on public finance or economics. Universities are slow to teach in new areas. Moreover, the study of social security straddles different academic disciplines. Part of the reason given for the relative neglect of social security in the secondary-school and university curricula of nearly all countries is that the study of social security does not lead to a clearly defined profession or career. But this is also true of many other subjects long taught in universities.

Research

156 The absence of a firm basis in university study results in a relative neglect of research. Compared with other subjects playing only a minor role in our economies, social security forms the subject of few theses and only a limited number of research-based books are written about it. This leads to the relative lack of discussion in the quality press and the concentration on relatively trivial issues in the popular papers. In economic discussions the cost of social security can easily be presented as a burden without proper consideration of the benefits given to individuals and of the social cohesion of society to which it makes such a major contribution. The impression is easily given that social security is a major consumer of resources, when in reality its major function is to redistribute rights to spend from those at work to those who, for a variety of reasons, are unable to work and from the healthy to those currently needing health care.

157 Because there is too little research, too little is known about public attitudes to social security and how consumers would like the system to be developed. Thus, decisions of major consequence are taken by the social partners or by governments without their knowing how far the priorities they have chosen are really in line with those of the workers and consumers whose money they ultimately are spending. Similarly, too little is known about the problems which individual consumers encounter when using social security. Of special importance is the extent to which rights which are legally available are actually used. However small the minority who do not receive what they are entitled to receive, the reasons for this failure need to be known and corrective action taken. Moreover, as studies of "take-up" rates have been conducted in more countries, the failure of some benefits, particularly means-tested benefits, to reach their target groups has been shown to be substantial. Rights which for any reason are not effectively exercised are paper rights—a failure for which social security institutions should take responsibility.

158 Social security institutions should sponsor research on social security both in research organisations and in universities. In some countries, it may be appropriate to endow chairs in social security at universities and to sponsor students by scholarships and other means. Much is to be gained by the study of social security on a comparative basis. We commend the comparative studies undertaken by international organisations and we *strongly recommend* the expansion of these comparative studies.

Bureaucracy and accessibility

159 Social security institutions are under bureaucratic pressure to streamline their procedures so as to increase the efficiency with which they perform their functions. But efficiency can be carried too far, if it fails to provide for the diversity of individual users and the special problems of minority groups. Public agencies can too easily come to be run for the convenience of administrators rather than as a service geared to the needs of every type of user. In this context, administrators see computer technology as a way of cutting costs, abolishing monotonous jobs and, through rapid information retrieval, giving the public a more reliable and speedier service. Some users of social security, however, view these developments with suspicion and anxiety. First, it is feared that by human error some of the information recorded on the computer may be wrong and that they will not know what is recorded about them. Second, they fear that they will obtain a less personal service, on the grounds that "You cannot argue with a computer." They receive standard answers to unstandardised questions and are denied the information and advice to which they feel they are entitled.

160 As mentioned earlier, in many countries social security has grown up on a fragmentary basis. There are often different arrangements for different benefits and different arrangements for different categories of workers and of the self-employed. Thus, each fund may have only a national administration and no branch offices to which the public has access. All this makes social security appear even more incomprehensible and inaccessible to the individual citizen. It leads to claimants being sent from office to office and adds to administrative costs.

161 The rational solution from the point of view of accessibility would be to unify the different arrangements and provide one office in each area which would be equipped to deal with any social security problem. There is a trend towards unification in a number of countries. There are, however, political obstacles to unification in many others. Occupational or industrial groups want to retain their own funds and resist the general pooling of risks. And it may be the case that a greater sense of solidarity, and thus willingness to pay contributions, is generated on an occupational basis than on a national basis. However desirable national solidarity may be in terms of equity and simplicity, people are more reluctant to pay to a national plan, because contributions come to be seen more as taxes, than to private occupational plans or to regional programmes (where they exist), where contributions are seen as insurance premiums. The answers to these questions no doubt vary between countries. One possible solution may be to have a national

minimum programme with occupational provision on top, as has developed in a number of countries. Thus, a basic element of equity is established but the sense of occupational solidarity is mobilised for further provision. But even where the unification of different systems is not acceptable, it should be possible for there to be area offices which can deal with all social security matters *on behalf of* the different institutions. Recent developments in communication technology would seem to have made possible what may not have been possible before.

162 We have set out in earlier chapters a whole series of desirable developments in social security for the period up to the year 2000. We accept that many of them will have to wait until the economic situation improves. But the types of development envisaged in this chapter are of a very different financial order. The working practices of social security institutions need to be improved to make them more responsive to individual needs and problems. Such improvements will not be costless, but they will cost much less than the provision of new rights and the upgrading of existing benefits. Thus we *recommend* that the issues raised in this chapter should be given especial attention in the immediate future.

Raising the level of public knowledge

163 We *recommend* that, in each country, social security institutions should make concerted efforts to improve the general knowledge of the public about social security—particularly as regards rights to benefits and where the money is spent. The aim should be both to help people to claim and to prevent abuse and the misuse of social security. In many countries, the responsibility for this activity may be best exercised by governments. Special educational material should be prepared for schools and a series of attractive information bulletins should be circulated to contributors. Particular attention should be paid to groups with special problems, such as illiterates, the disabled and those with inadequate command of the official language(s). Social security institutions should take special steps to develop close working relationships with the media, and to provide appropriate material according to the readership of newspapers and the character of particular television programmes. In some countries, institutions will need to finance jointly a central information bureau to carry out these functions.

Area offices

164 We *recommend* that area offices should be established at which all social security matters can be handled—on behalf of different institutions in countries where unification cannot be achieved.

Responding to questions about individual rights

165 People have a right to know about their own personal expectations from social security. Questions such as "What will my old age pension be when I am 65?", "What would my wife and children receive if I died tomorrow?", "How much will I get if I do not recover and become long-term disabled?", should be answered promptly and as simply as possible, either orally or in writing. It is not enough to respond to such inquiries with a leaflet explaining how benefits in general are calculated, or to refer people to laws and regulations which most people cannot understand. The more complex a pension formula is, the more people need to have their questions answered. Inevitably, assumptions will often have to be made in giving answers. To be told that, if you go on earning as you are now, you will get a specific sum of money per month, and that, if prices go up, your pension will go up with them, is a sufficient answer for most purposes. Moreover, social security institutions should send periodic statements about accumulated rights to pensions, where they exist, to all insured persons.

166 We *recommend* that social security institutions should equip themselves to provide reasonably prompt answers

to reasonable inquiries from individuals about their personal entitlements, at area offices or in writing, and provide regular statements on accumulated rights to pensions where they exist.

Handicapped claimants

167 Forms and letters sent out by social security institutions
are generally too complex for those with limited education
to be able to understand. Offices are often inaccessible to disabled
people, and communications with blind people are not generally
provided in Braille. Ethnic minorities and migrant workers with
limited command of the local language often face great difficulties
in their contacts with social security institutions.

168 We *recommend:*

(a) that organised systems of expert assistance should be established to assist people to fill in applications and to explain the
contents of forms and letters;

(b) that social security offices should all provide inquiry counters
which are readily accessible to disabled people in wheelchairs;

(c) that communications should be in Braille with blind people
who have learned to use it; and

(d) that special measures should be taken for communications with
persons without an effective knowledge of the official lan-
guage(s).

Social security law

169 We *recommend* that dispersed social security laws should
be integrated and possibly consolidated, and that the legislation should be drafted in the clearest possible language.

Complaints procedure

170 People should have a clear right to make complaints about
the way they have been treated by any social security institution. If such complainants remain unsatisfied in a complaints

procedure which should be available within the institution itself, they should be dealt with by an independent authority.

171 We *recommend* that, in the absence of administrative review by a judge or independent appeal board, one possibility is for complaints to be handled by an ombudsman: there may well be a case for an ombudsman specialising in social security matters.

The right of appeal

172 In paragraph 170 we said that at the first stage a complaint should be handled by some available process within the institution itself. But if the complainant is still left dissatisfied, it is not enough to provide an independent right of appeal without making sure that people know of its existence and how to use it.

173 We *recommend* that all written notifications that a benefit has been granted, refused or changed should include, in simple language, an explanation of how and where to make a complaint and to an appeal, and how to obtain legal or other help in making it, free of charge.

174 The procedure on appeal should not be delayed; it should be inquisitorial (non-adversarial) rather than adversarial, avoid undue formality, and enable a claimant to appear on his own behalf or be represented by some person of his own choosing; he should be given the benefit of any reasonable doubt. As far as possible, the process should be free of charge.

Privacy

175 People should be reassured that information about them will not be given to third parties (other than other social security institutions and social services). This right to privacy should be unambiguous and breaches should be punishable. Special precautions are needed to safeguard information kept on computers.

176 We *recommend* that it should be made illegal for social security institutions to reveal any information about individuals to third parties without their consent, unless specifically provided for in the law.

Access to personal files and rights to a hearing

177 We recommend that everyone should have access, under appropriate procedures, to their personal files in social security offices, the right to request changes, and the right to a fair hearing and prompt decision where they have a reasonable interest.

Advances and the payment of interest

178 We *recommend* that, where there is delay in establishing the precise level of a benefit, the claimant should be entitled to receive an advance and interest on any sum not paid on time. When an overpayment has been made, the beneficiary should be given reasonable time to repay.

Participation

179 In many countries, the social partners (representatives of employers and workers) have played an important role in the establishment and administration of social security. It is important that this participation, which takes different forms in different countries, should be continued. But there is a growing demand that representatives of groups of claimants, such as the aged, one-parent families or the disabled, should be given a similar role in the advisory machinery and/or administration of social security. In addition, claims are made for a parallel role for the employees of social security institutions.

180 We *recommend* that social security institutions should widen the basis of participation in their advisory machinery and administration according to particular national situations.

Annual reports

181 We *recommend* that each social security institution should be required to publish a comprehensive annual report on its administration, including a statement of income and expenditure in accordance with accepted accounting principles.

Conclusion

182 Our recommendations are essentially aimed at making social security institutions more customer-conscious—more responsible to the varying requirements of their users. There is always a danger that any public institution, particularly a monopoly institution not faced with market competition, will put bureaucratic considerations ahead of responsiveness to human beings. If social security institutions become impenetrable bureaucratic fortresses, speaking only in their own incomprehensible language, the public are bound to seek other mechanisms which will respond quickly and sympathetically to their needs. It is partly because of the inefficiencies of some social security institutions that moves to substitute private systems for public systems have generated considerable public support.

Chapter 6

The financing of social security

183 As pointed out in Chapter 1, criticism of social security is heavily concentrated on its cost and the damaging social and economic effects which are said to arise from its financing. We have argued in earlier chapters that social security, as we interpret it, is not yet fully developed in any country. While we see ways in which the prospective growth in costs might be moderated in some countries (e.g. in health care), we do not see any acceptable means for major reductions in expenditure. On the contrary, we believe that social security should be extended in a number of important directions as national economies recover from the current recession. Are there, therefore, ways in which the financing of social security can be changed so that it is paid for in more acceptable ways? Does a greater role for the private sector offer a solution to current problems? And if so, in which fields?

184 Some would argue that social security could have more favourable effects on economies if pay-as-you-go financing were abandoned and the stern actuarial disciplines of full capital funding were reintroduced. Thus, social security would contribute to savings which could be channelled directly or indirectly into real investment which would in turn promote the economic growth needed to meet the likely increase in cost. We do not accept this argument. First, accurate funding is not practicable when long-term benefits are indexed. Second, funding would increase the problems of tax resistance in the short and medium term. Third, investment is limited by profitable investment opportunities rather than by the availability of savings. If savings are, at any time, too low to finance investment, the adjustment could be made by fiscal means when this is required. Fourth, we do not regard it as proven that savings in the economy as a whole are necessarily reduced by the pay-as-you-go financing of social security programmes. In many countries, the growth of pay-as-you-go-financed social security has been accompanied by an unprecedented boom in a variety of different forms of saving. Fifth, whether social security benefits are financed by a funded or by a pay-as-you-go system, it is the current year's workers, employers, consumers and taxpayers who must provide the funds for the current year's beneficiaries. This year's benefits under the pay-as-you-go system are financed from this year's contributions and this year's taxes. In a funded system, this year's benefits are financed from this year's contributions and from this year's interest on past investments; this year's interest is paid by this year's taxpayers (in the case of investments in government or municipal bonds) or by this year's consumers through higher prices or rents (in the case of corporate bonds, mortgages or property holdings). In both systems, those now working, consuming and paying taxes must give up a portion of their incomes to provide incomes for social security beneficiaries. However, for reasons of prudence and liquidity, it is always desirable to have a reserve fund under the pay-as-you-go system of financing.

185 There is at present a remarkable diversity in the ways in which social security is financed in different countries. Some rely almost exclusively on tax financing, whilst others rely very much on earmarked contributions paid by the self-employed, employees and employers, often with the major burden being borne by the employers. Where this last pattern of financing is applied, employers complain that the social security contributions which they are made to pay make their products uncompetitive in world markets, particularly in the labour-intensive industries, thus sharpening the current recession and the consequential high level of unemployment. Financing by contributions is also attacked in social terms as being an unfair burden on low earners, creating or exacerbating poverty among the low paid. Where general tax financing has been adopted, the complaint is about the intolerable levels of taxation and its adverse social and economic effects. Are there social or economic considerations pointing towards either alternative?

Economic effects

186 We are well aware that employers feel that the high social security contributions they are compelled to pay raise their costs of production and thus reduce their competitiveness with pro-

ducers in countries where employers do not have to pay such contributions or else pay them at a much lower level. Thus, it is argued that high social security contributions are in part responsible for the present high level of unemployment in industrialised countries. This question has been extensively studied in a number of countries. While it is true that employers might achieve a short-term gain if these contributions were lowered, it is not likely that this gain would be sustained in the longer term. What was gained in lower contributions is likely to be paid out sooner or later in higher wages and salaries or in other wage costs. If the argument were sound, countries within the European Community with low social security contributions would, over the years, have made great gains at the expense of countries with high social security contributions. But this does not appear to have happened as a matter of history. The essential point is that it is total labour costs which affect competitiveness, and social security contributions are only part of those costs. International comparisons do not support the argument that there is any significant connection between social security contributions and high total labour costs.

187 Is it true that higher employers' contributions particularly damage labour-intensive firms and encourage the replacement of labour with capital? First, it should be pointed out that firms making capital goods also have to pay the same high employers' contributions. Capital-intensive firms pay high employers' contributions indirectly on their raw materials, plant and energy. Second, high employers' contributions may well cause cash wages to be lower than would otherwise be the case, so that total labour costs are not, in fact, increased by employers' contributions. Third, in so far as high employers' contributions encourage all firms to use more capital-intensive methods of production, this applies to labour-intensive firms as well. This encouragement of investment may lead them to produce at lower cost and thus to be more competitive in world markets. For these reasons, the argument has little credibility.

188 It is sometimes suggested that the employers' contribution should be levied on added value rather than on payroll. But this could bring both depreciation and profits into the assessment and would discourage investment. Added value has limited coverage; it cannot be assessed in many fields of public employment.

189 While there is no clear evidence that employers' contributions as a whole are bad for employment, the presence of a relatively low ceiling on employers' contributions may damage employment. It discourages offers of part-time jobs and encourages firms to lengthen working hours and to prefer overtime working to taking on further workers. And by increasing the relative cost of unskilled workers, it discourages firms from employing them.

190 Apart from this point about the ceiling, we are not convinced that there are compelling economic arguments for choosing any particular form of financing statutory social security. All systems of taxation have effects on the economy. It is therefore somewhat unreal to examine one particular way of raising money without looking at the total effects of all ways of raising money in a particular country at a particular time. Thus, each national context should be considered separately. As economic arguments are not decisive, the issue can be judged simply on social, psychological and political considerations.

Social effects

191 The case for financing by contributions rather than taxes is based on the following considerations:

1. Contributions impose a discipline on those who pay and on legislators and administrators to prevent irresponsible increases in benefits.
2. Where there are distinct funds, it is possible for those concerned to participate in running them.

3. Where there are funds, they help to secure that commitments to pay benefits, particularly long-term benefits, are honoured.

4. By charging the cost of benefits on labour costs, employers have, in theory at least, incentives to prevent risks arising.

5. Contributions are administratively easy to collect.

6. Only by earmarked contributions can the payment of earnings-related benefits be socially justified. They become in effect deferred wages.

7. When funds are accumulated, they can be used for public investment.

8. Employees may be more willing to pay a contribution related to benefits which they can draw than general taxation.

192 The case for financing by general taxation rather than contributions is based on the following considerations:

1. Flat-rate contributions are highly regressive.

2. Where there is a ceiling on earnings-related contributions, they are regressive. Even where there is no ceiling, proportional contributions are less fair than progressive taxes on income.

3. Contributions can create or exacerbate poverty among low earners.

4. Contributions exclude persons with pronounced social needs.

5. Contributions are not levied on investment income.

6. Taxation enables governments to assess priorities between all fields of public expenditure, including education, the environment, measures to combat unemployment, etc. This may mean that benefits promised earlier can be modified in the light of new priorities.

7. In so far as tax financing leads to administration by government, it leads to greater co-ordination between services, e.g. health, social welfare and employment services. Moreover, responsibility can be decentralised to local democratically elected bodies which raise a considerable part of their own revenue.

193 It is not necessarily the case that tax financing places less of a burden on those with low incomes. It depends where extra taxes are levied to pay for social security. For example, extra taxes on tobacco might fall more heavily on low earners than social security contributions, though the incidence is less visible. An extra yield from income tax may be secured by lowering the threshold to bring low earners into the tax net. Moreover, it is possible to relieve the regressiveness of social security contributions by tax concessions or refunds for low earners.

194 The strongest case for contributions is where benefits are earnings-related. Moreover, participation in the management of the programme may encourage willingness to pay. The strongest case for tax financing is where it is particularly desired to cover everyone—for example, for family allowances or health care. Tax financing can also be used to pay minimum flat-rate benefits to all, leaving earnings-related contributions to pay for earnings-related benefits on top.

195 The choices made in particular countries will inevitably depend on balancing all these considerations, and all countries are inevitably strongly influenced by their historical experience. This limits the political possibilities of radical change. In general, however, we *recommend* progressive rather than regressive ways of financing social security. The largest single benefit is pensions, and it is the lower income groups which are least likely to live long enough to draw them. Regressive financing leads to the socially unacceptable result of the poor paying for the pensions of the rich. Partly for this reason, we believe that contribution ceilings for earnings-related benefits should be abolished. In addition, as mentioned above, if the ceilings are relatively low, they are damaging to employment and lead to discrimination against unskilled workers among whom unemployment is most heavily concentrated. We accept, however, that when earnings-related contributions are used to finance flat-rate benefits, it would seem unreasonable for there to be no ceiling. We *recommend* that a reasonable and appropriate portion of public contributory social security programmes be financed in part from the more progressive tax sources of the nation. We do not believe such general revenue financing should adversely affect the entitlement to benefits as a matter of contributory or statutory right, or imply the necessity for the application of any income or assets test for claiming benefits.

196 In looking ahead for the period up to the year 2000, we believe that the question of providing for those who have not entered the working population will come into increasing prominence. It is, moreover, central to the question of poverty. If, as we believe, a solution should be found to this problem, it will require a greater element of tax financing. But it does not necessarily involve the dismantling of existing programmes. Either government contributions can be used to give rights to those not covered on a contributory basis, or some form of minimum income guarantee (either associated with income tax or not) can be superimposed on contributory programmes. We expect different countries to find different ways of resolving this problem. The question of financing is critical to the recommendations made earlier about the extension of social security to persons not covered or inadequately covered at present.

Increasing the role of the private sector

197 Can a solution be found by increasing the role of the private sector? The relationship between the public sector and the private sector is complex and can take a variety of forms. The following list gives examples of the various forms found in different countries:

1. *Subsidy.* Private insurance arrangements or non-profit voluntary associations which meet certain conditions may be subsidised.
2. *The requirement to provide.* Legislation may require employers to provide benefits (e.g. a proportion of pay for the first few weeks of sickness or a redundancy payment on termination of employment). There may be public subsidy.

3. *The requirement to insure.* Employers may be required to insure against a defined risk (e.g. industrial/occupational accidents) but may choose their insurer. There may be competition between public and private insurers.

4. *Contracting out.* An employer, union or insurance company providing cover no less favourable than that provided by a public programme may be allowed to contract insured persons out of a public programme.

5. *Unregulated supplementary insurance.* This may be provided by profit or non-profit organisations, such as mutual aid societies.

6. *Regulated supplementary insurance.* Regulations may cover policies on investment, submission of accounts, etc.

7. *Tax incentives.* Employee and/or employer contributions may be allowed free of income tax or corporation tax. Invested funds may be free of income tax. Tax incentives can be given:

   (a) free of regulations; or

   (b) subject to regulations specifying the maximum premiums that are allowed tax free for particular individuals or under conditions which insurance or pension programmes are required to meet in order to claim the tax exemption (vesting, portability, equal rights for men and women and how they are defined, inclusion of survivors' benefits, provision for divorced dependants, provision for a specified rate of price inflation, etc.).

8. *Use of private service providers by public agencies.* Many public health insurance plans pay private hospitals and private professionals for services or reimburse insured persons who have purchased services from private providers.

198 We are in no doubt, first, that subsidised non-profit voluntary associations can play an important role in providing particular types of services and should be encouraged. Second, whatever level of provision is made by statutory insurance, there

will be room for supplementary insurance on top either to provide a higher level of protection or to meet special requirements of particular occupational groups. A more contentious question is whether private pension programmes should be given tax concessions. The case in favour of concessions is that this additional saving should be encouraged. The case against it is that such further saving is likely to benefit the higher income groups and that the income tax base is eroded, leaving higher burdens to be carried by other people. The argument that pensions will be taxed when such plans pay them out does not offset the gains that would result if both contributions and the income of funds were free of tax. In many cases, the precedent of tax subsidy was established before there was a fully developed social security programme. Most of us believe that, in principle, such tax concessions are unwarranted. All of us recognise, however, that they cannot be abolished at the stroke of the pen. We *recommend* unanimously that means should be found of placing strict limits on them. The majority of us would go further and aim eventually to abolish them. At the very least, the majority *recommend* that the interest earned by non-governmental funds should be taxed.

199 In the case of requirements on employers to provide benefits, we see no objection to this approach, provided that the security granted is absolute. Special arrangements may be needed to safeguard the position of employees whose employers go bankrupt—either by the government underwriting such provision or by some system of insurance against this eventuality. It should, however, be pointed out that, though such arrangements may be technically private expenditure, the effect is the same as if they were public expenditure. They reduce compulsorily the amount that earners have in their pay packets or cheques, and they do nothing to relieve the problem of tax resistance.

200 A more difficult question is whether part of basic social security protection should be provided by private insurers, either by a requirement on employers to insure or by a provision which allows contracting out.

201 The case for the use of private insurers is based on the following arguments:

1. Competition between insurers will ensure efficiency in dealing with claims.
2. In health insurance, competition between insurers will lead to efficiency in the use of health resources. The insurer who can provide a package of quality health care which gives consumer satisfaction at low cost will attract the business.
3. In pension insurance, private insurers have to accommodate funds for investment, and this adds to saving. Such plans cannot be run on a pay-as-you-go basis like public programmes which dissipate potential savings.
4. Private pension funds prevent the concentration of too much control of investment in public or bureaucratic hands.
5. Private pension funds have the flexibility to meet the particular needs of specific firms, industries or occupations.

202 The case against the use of private insurers is based on the following arguments:

1. Competitive insurance necessarily involves taking account of profit and administrative costs, including such matters as legal charges and sales promotion, which are able to be avoided in publicly run plans. This offsets any extra efficiency in dealing with claims, which anyway may not be a major consideration with employers who place the business. In various countries, administrative costs and profit absorb 40 per cent of premiums; quite often, they even exceed 50 per cent.
2. A different economic problem arises from the need for private insurers to anticipate all future contingencies when calculating premiums. In paragraph 106 we spoke of the added cost of upgrading benefits to the workers' compensation level if the

undesirable demarcation between work and other incapacity is to be removed. Many workers' compensation programmes are supported by private insurance plans, and these must be funded, as we say, to meet all future contingencies from current annual premiums. Among the special contingencies to be covered is the uncertain factor of inflation. Even by itself, the need to provide for this can cause total annual demands, in the form of premiums, which are much greater than the cost would be to the community of a pay-as-you-go system handled by the public sector. Clearly, the public sector choice would enable some degree of upgrading without any additional cost.

3. On health insurance, even if employers and consumers can be given incentives to be cost-conscious in the choice of policy, neither is in a good position to judge value for money. It opens the door for fly-by-night insurers who are out to cut costs by refusing to provide necessary health care where consumers are unlikely to be aware of this refusal.

4. If the accumulation of funds for pension insurance is desirable, this could also be done by public insurers, and their investments could readily be channelled in directions which are socially and economically useful. We regard the argument that pay-as-you-go financing reduces total savings as unproven.

5. In occupational injury, competition leads insurers to try and secure out-of-court settlements for serious cases which are substantially below what the claim is worth, to dispute claims and to spend a high proportion of their funds on legal costs rather than on meeting claims. On the other hand, small claims may be settled on terms which are over-generous in order to avoid administrative costs. This is socially undesirable. In addition, the system can involve inordinate delay and throws heavy legal costs on to the claimant or on to the system of legal aid.

6. Private insurance reduces national solidarity. Those with low risks get favourable terms for insurance. Those with high risks get unfavourable terms.

7. Private insurers can go bankrupt and thus fail to provide complete security.

203 On balance, we believe that the scales are clearly weighted against the use of private insurers, provided that public programmes are run efficiently and that they set out to make themselves responsive to user requirements. It is for this reason that we have included a whole section on this subject. In recent years a new proposal for financing health care under social security has attracted widespread interest in North America. Social security would give covered persons a voucher of a stated money value which they could present to an insurer of their choice. All insurers participating in this arrangement would have to cover the major contingencies and take all comers: they could not select good risks and refuse to take bad risks. Persons covered would have an incentive to find insurers who offered good value for money by offering the right to a cash refund if their policy cost less than the value of their voucher. Insurers would have an incentive to devise policies which offered what consumers wanted. There is no experience to show whether such a system would give the results claimed for it, nor whether the objections raised have real substance. In countries where attempts to regulate the health care system have not been effective, this may be an option to be investigated further. We accept also that, where occupational pension plans have become extensively developed before a second tier of earnings-related pensions has been established as part of basic protection, a contracting-out provision may have to be conceded politically to establish this second tier. As we said in Chapter 2, we consider the ends to be more important than the means. Some compromise of principle—in this case, uniformity—may be necessary to achieve the primary objective of full basic protection. The best can be the enemy of the good. But we do not consider it desirable public policy to allow an employer, union or insurance company to contract insured persons out of a public system. Contracting out augments administrative costs, increases the benefit costs for the coverage of those who are

not contracted out, and breaks the solidarity of the social security programme. We *recommend* that contracting out should not be permitted.

204 But the use of the private sector does nothing to relieve the problem of tax resistance. Indeed, it may make it worse in so far as the administrative costs and full funding requirements of private insurance involve greater costs. If employers withhold money which might alternatively have been in the pay cheque or packet for private social security contributions, this money is not available to pay taxes and public social security contributions. People still feel that they are not left with as much money as they want for their daily expenses. We accept that the logic of this argument could lead to the prohibition of employers' supplementary plans. But we consider that such a step would be inconsistent with the freedoms of a democratic society. But the point we make is that both statutory programmes and employers' plans contribute to what expresses itself as tax resistance.

Conclusion

205 Thus we see no magic formula which will provide a solution for the financing of social security. Nor is this surprising. The issue has long been debated, and over the past years possible alternatives have been intensively examined in many countries.

206 In our view, the problem of the cost of social security is essentially psychological and therefore becomes a matter for political decision. It is this that limits the level of contributions which are acceptable, rather than any economic considerations. There comes a point at which people believe that they are paying too much, whether they are paying this in the form of taxes or contributions, and no matter to whom such taxes are paid or by whose authority contributions are extracted. People see the benefits that social security will provide as remote, and tend to underestimate their own risks. Man is essentially a risk-taking animal. To some

extent this problem can be countered by public education—to bring
home to people the reality of the risks and the substantial benefits
which they obtain from social security in all its forms, and the cost
of providing these benefits. If young people today faced up to what
it would cost them to support their parents and pay bills for health
and social care for themselves and their families, public awareness
of the advantages of social security would be increased. It is for
this reason, among others, that we argued in Chapter 5 for a much
greater public relations effort by social security institutions.

207 As regards the immediate so-called "crisis" in social
security, two further points should be made and stressed.
First, the current "crisis" has not been caused mainly by the steady
increase in the number of pensioners nor by the gradual application
of technological improvements in medicine. It has been caused,
above all else, by lower rates of economic growth and heavy unemployment. In several countries, over a tenth of the labour force has,
within a few years, come to be a charge on social security funds
and therefore over a tenth of the labour force has ceased to pay
social security contributions, substantially lowered their contributions to general taxation and created deficits in a number of public
utility services which governments have had to finance. These costs
of unemployment amount to more than the cost of social-security-
financed health care in some countries. It is this extra burden, on
a scale for which social security funds were not designed to provide,
that is at the root of current problems of financing.

208 Second, it is grossly unfair to choose social security as the
scapegoat and ignore the growth of all other sectors of
public expenditure and of private plans. For example, over the past
30 years the share of education in the gross domestic product of
some industrialised societies has risen to a similar extent to health
care. In a number of countries, defence has been taking an
increasing share of the resources. It is the combination of all sectors
of public expenditure—education, international security and all

other sectors, as well as social security—that is contributing to the current problem of tax resistance.

209 In so far as there is a crisis in social security, it is a crisis not of the structure of social security but of the erosion of the economic base for its operation. *Social security is neither the cause of the crisis nor the cause of the recession.* To a considerable extent, social security has moderated both the economic and the social effects of the latter. Social security is blamed when employers see cuts in wage costs as necessary to restore profitability and to increase their competitiveness. Focusing on their heavy contributions to social security seems a strategy with greater prospects of success than a direct attack on the larger element of the cash wage.

210 The positive role of social security protection should always be remembered. In both health and social welfare, it has a large potential for creating both meaningful and socially useful jobs, particularly for women. Indeed, the public sector as a whole has done much (and could do more) to create more equal earnings for men and women, as it is in the public sector that senior jobs for women are particularly to be found. The present psychological resistance to paying for social security is due to the rapidity with which payments for social security have increased in a period of slow growth or no growth. Over a longer period and in a more favourable economic climate, such growth would not have been the cause of criticism except from a doctrinaire minority.

211 In selecting priorities for each stage of development over the next two decades, careful choices will need to be made to achieve a balance within programmes and between programmes. In our view, in making these choices those developments which benefit the poorest should have early attention.

Chapter 7

Summary and recommendations

The background

212 The language and form of this report was necessarily reached by consensus, except where otherwise indicated. At the same time, it should be emphasised that our collective and individual experience, which has been gained in different countries and against a background of different responsibilities, has been brought to bear on the subject, and that the report takes that experience fully into account. It has been based, as well, upon the wisdom of various national and international organisations and the valuable work of the International Labour Office.

213 We believe that the report presents a bold and admittedly controversial attempt to indicate the future trends of social security policy which should and could arise in the next two decades. It presents both a challenge and an opportunity to social security policy-makers and to students of the subject. However, it is probable that new developments will occur which cannot be foreseen at present. There is clearly a need for a periodic reappraisal of any attempt to pierce the future.

214 We *recommend,* therefore, that the Director-General of the International Labour Office establish an administrative mechanism to monitor formally, at regular intervals, the recommendations and commentary in this report. We believe that at least every five years such a body should be given the responsibility of re-examining these recommendations and submitting a report thereon, which should then become the basis for further widespread international review, discussion and critical analysis.

215 Social security today is under attack from opposite camps. On the one hand, it is accused of aggravating the world economic crisis by reducing saving, cutting investment, aggravating inflation, augmenting unemployment and undermining incentives to work. On the other hand, it is blamed for failing to solve the problems of poverty, for discriminating against women, for not

treating equally those with similar needs and for distorting social priorities. Thus, while some press for a fundamental reorientation of social security policies, others argue that the whole system should be dismantled as it is no longer needed in societies which have reached their present level of affluence. No longer is there a clear consensus favouring further developments.

216 The cost of social security has been rapidly increasing, not only because of developments in coverage of both persons and risks but also because of the maturing of pension systems, the ageing of the population, the growth of family break-up and technological developments in medicine. On top of all this, the present acute recession has imposed further heavy burdens: not only has cash support to be given to those without jobs, but also the funds from which to provide this support have been eroded by the loss of contribution and tax income from unemployed persons. The maturing of pension programmes, the increasing proportion of elderly and further technological developments are all factors which may increase costs still further in the future. These costs could readily be met if unemployment declined and a reasonable rate of economic growth were once more attained.

Assumptions about the future

217 In making this report we have had to make assumptions about the future. A key assumption underlying our report is that over the period up to the year 2000 there will be a resumption of economic growth sufficient to secure a substantial reduction in unemployment. We do not, however, assume growth rates as high as those of the 1950s and 1960s. We expect the increase in jobs to come mainly in service occupations. Among them, services for health and social welfare will need to be expanded. Thus, developments in social security can contribute to overcoming the present economic crisis if acceptable means can be found to finance them or if the psychological resistance to paying for them can be overcome.

218 We have no way of knowing whether the present trend towards new life-styles and the break-up of marriages will continue or whether there will be a return to earlier patterns of behaviour. But we consider it right to try and adapt social security to provide for these new life-styles. Similarly, we cannot predict the future trend in prices but it seems right to provide for inflation at rates which cannot be predicted in advance.

The aims of social security

219 The fundamental aim of social security is to give individuals and families the confidence that their level of living and quality of life will not, in so far as possible, be greatly eroded by *any* social or economic eventuality. This involves not merely meeting needs as they arise but also preventing risks from arising in the first place and helping individuals and families to make the best possible adjustment when they are faced with disabilities and disadvantages which have not been, and could not be, prevented. To achieve these aims, not only cash benefits but also a wide range of services are required. We *recommend* as a central aim that persons currently not protected or inadequately protected should be fully covered where it has not been possible to prevent the contingency or its continuance (paragraph 42).

220 Among the risks which tend to be inadequately provided for at present are those of legal costs, of certain educational costs for mature students and of arbitrary eviction from home or farm or of arbitrary dismissal from employment.

221 We do not accept that greater affluence makes the provision of social security any less necessary. As a society becomes richer, a higher proportion of income is needed to protect it against the key risks of pensions and health care, if only because of longer periods of retirement and survival to higher ages. Private insurance against some other risks such as unemployment and long-term health and social care is not available. In general, the richer people are, the greater protection they seem to seek. Neither is it practi-

cable nor acceptable wholly to replace universal rights with selective (income-tested) rights. This would lead to poor services for poor people and the polarisation of society into those with generous employer-based provisions for security and those with nothing other than stigmatised residual provision with inadequate levels of claiming or "take-up". In many countries, there is at present no room for a further income-tested programme on top of existing income-tested provisions without creating very serious disincentives to work or save.

222 We *recommend* that at least a significant element of earnings-related provision is desirable (paragraph 51).

223 We *recommend* that private pension plans should be required to improve arrangements for the transfer of pension rights between plans, or for the full protection of acquired rights and plan solvency, and that they should include some element of inflation protection for pensions in payment; furthermore, private pension plans should be regulated with these ultimate aims in view (paragraph 52).

224 We *recommend* that the long-term aim should be to ensure that the minimum benefit paid to those not at work should provide a level of living of at least half the average net disposable income per head, adjusted for families of different composition (paragraph 53).

225 In the case of statutory pension rights we *recommend* that pensions in payment should be related to an index of earnings or gross domestic product per head (paragraph 54).

226 All except one of us *recommend* that building an effective minimum income for all residents should be accepted as the major challenge for social security policy to be achieved before the year 2000 (paragraph 60). We all agree that the persistence of poverty in affluent societies is particularly intolerable. The poor have a right to an acceptable quality of life which enables them to participate fully in the society of the country in which they live. One of us strongly disagrees with the recommendation for a minimum income as a way to fight poverty.

International action

227 We *recommend,* in connection with the movement of persons between countries, that continued efforts should be made to take advantage of the framework for co-ordination of national social security arrangements outlined in the Conventions and Recommendations adopted on this subject by the International Labour Conference. Further, we *recommend* that international action be pursued to enlarge the network of bilateral and multilateral agreements and to achieve between them a greater measure of compatibility and co-ordination (paragraph 70).

228 In relation to the harmonisation of systems of social security, we *recommend* that further efforts should be made by international action to explore areas of social security provision in respect of which further harmonisation would be feasible (paragraph 73).

Developments in cash benefits

229 While strict insurance-based arrangements for social security have the advantage that the revenue is on the whole readily collected, they have social disadvantages as often constituted at present. Those who cannot earn because of disability or handicap and those who cannot get established or re-established in the labour market are excluded. Those caring for children or the disabled or infirm and those who adopt new quasi-marital lifestyles or whose marriages or other partnerships break up are penalised. On the other hand, some survivors may be compensated for a financial loss which has not occurred.

230 In planning for the future, we *recommend* (paragraph 83) that policies should be based on the following principles:

1. It is a denial of a basic human right and quite unacceptable to treat women by reason of their sex less favourably than men, or men less favourably than women.

2. Persons, whether married or not, who live together should each have benefits in their own right rather than be treated as dependants, whether of their husbands or any other person; and their partners should, where necessary, pay contributions to secure them out of their income.

3. Where rights are derived from contribution or earnings records or years of insurance, each year of right acquired by persons who live together should be shared between that couple, with benefits paid separately so that neither is deprived of self-support, and enhanced where necessary to secure an acceptable minimum.

4. Absence from the labour force for child-rearing or for the care of the disabled or infirm should be socially recognised by allowances or benefits and, where applicable, by credits towards contributory insurance.

5. The aim should be to recognise all types of couples who are sharing income when building up rights to social security.

231 Thus we *favour* credits for periods spent caring for children or infirm or disabled persons, or better still, allowances for these responsibilities out of which contributions can be paid.

232 We *recommend* that provisions for widowed mothers' benefits should be extended to either survivor of a partnership but should be recast to reflect the relative past earnings of the parties to the partnership (paragraph 93).

233 Similarly, in relation to survivors who are under pension age and without dependent children, benefit amounts *should reflect* relative past earnings of the two parties, in such a way as to prevent financial compensation for loss which has not occurred (paragraph 95). None the less, where such assistance is necessary, we *recommend* that a benefit should be paid for a suffi-

cient time to enable the survivor to reorganise his or her life, to take vocational training and to look for paid work (paragraph 95).

234 We *recommend* that there should be much more extensive provision of training and retraining allowances, not only for women re-entering the labour force but also for workers or others with redundant skills or disability. After these allowances, unemployment benefit should be payable. The majority of us believe that part-time work should be covered by unemployment insurance and that, where unemployment benefits are paid, they should be of unlimited duration, subject to the removal, after a period, of the "suitable work" constraint and to the possibility of a reduction in the level of benefits where these are high in relation to potential earnings (paragraph 99).

235 We *recommend* that countries should explore the possibility of, and endeavour to implement, public employment programmes which will enable these people to retain their work skills and to achieve something for themselves and for the community (paragraph 101).

236 The majority of us *recommend* that countries should progress towards unified systems of disability benefits based on degree rather than on cause of disability, as resources permit and as public opinion comes to accept the justice of the case. The minority, while not opposing unification, would retain extra compensation for workers injured in the course of their employment (paragraph 107).

237 In our view, old-age insurance is the wrong instrument to use for attempts to alleviate the current crisis (e.g. by lowering the pension age). We *recommend* that the employer should be required to prove that a worker is no longer able to do any work which he can offer before he can impose retirement (paragraph 115). We also *recommend* that employees and the self-employed should be given the right to reduce their weekly working time, with a corresponding reduction in earnings, as they get older (paragraph 116). They should be entitled to part pension during this transition period. In general, we believe that there is a strong case for the pension being higher when elderly people become infirm and need the assistance of others.

Developments in services

238 We are in no doubt that the development of services for prevention and rehabilitation should be given the highest priority in social security policy for the period up to the year 2000 and beyond. This development should take place not just in health policy but also in employment policy, family and population policy and social welfare policies. We believe this because of the contribution which can be made to the quality of life. Co-ordinated action is needed by virtually all departments of government, employers and employees, voluntary bodies, families and individuals. The priority for prevention should also be carried through into priorities for research, particularly in the social sciences.

Health services

239 We have listed in our report the many factors which have been causing the escalation of health care costs in so many countries. Several of these are bound to continue. It would be undesirable to limit medical progress or restrict access to the benefits or medical technology which can *demonstrably* improve the quality of life (paragraph 129).

240 But the greatly increased spending on health care and the extension of social security over the past 30 years have not resulted in an accelerated decline in mortality rates as a whole; nor have they narrowed relative gaps in the health status between socio-economic groups. Spending more on curative services does not necessarily bring better health. Among the reasons for this are the relative neglect of preventive action in its widest sense, the wasteful use of health resources and the lack of community participation.

Moreover, while there are powerful incentives for any medical activities which might possibly improve the quality of life and postpone death, social welfare action which can contribute to the same objectives tends to operate on a limited budget, to be underfinanced and, in some countries, to carry a stigma and to be subject to financial barriers.

241 We *recommend* that priorities should be increasingly asserted over the coming years to achieve the more cost-effective use of health services, to change the balance between curative action and preventive action and between medically authorised action and socially authorised action and to enable people to play a greater role in decision-making about their own health and social care (paragraph 132).

242 We recognise that this recommendation will require the modification of certain established traditions and freedoms in the provision of health services. This is inevitable. The aim should be to use the level of staff and the level of scientific and administrative technology appropriate to the particular task. One of the means of securing this is a system of primary health care based on the principles established at the UNICEF/WHO Conference at Alma-Ata in 1978 (paragraph 139).

Social services

243 We *recommend* that there should be a major development of social services in the period up to the year 2000. There should be a right of *access* to social services as they are developed and in a practical sense become available, parallel to the right of *access* to health services, without prohibitive financial barriers. Social services should be co-ordinated locally to provide comprehensive help and support and continuity of care to families and individuals. This should be a responsibility of government in consultation with interested groups (paragraphs 147-149).

244   We *recommend* that mechanisms should be established to
secure community and non-profit agency participation in
the planning and running of local health and social welfare services
(paragraph 150).

Relations with the public and the administration

245   Social security has grown to a vast size in a fog of public
ignorance about it. Misunderstandings are widespread and
give rise to the exploitation of public prejudices. Social security
lacks a firm base in education at any level and is relatively
neglected as a subject for university research. Social security institutions should sponsor such research. Much is to be gained by the
study of social security on a comparative basis. Whilst commending
international organisations for their activities in this direction, we
strongly recommend that these studies be expanded (paragraph 158).

246   Bureaucratic pressures for efficiency can be carried too far
if they result in the depersonalisation of services to users
and the neglect of the special needs of minorities. Where social
security is fragmented and programmes have only a national
administration, the system can easily be seen as inaccessible and
incomprehensible by the citizens for whose benefit it has been
designed. We *recommend* that these issues should be given especial
attention in the immediate future (paragraph 162).

247   We *recommend* that, in each country, social security institutions should make concerted efforts to improve the general knowledge of the public about social security—particularly
as regards rights to benefit and where the money is spent (paragraph 163). Special attention should be paid to the problem
of illiterates, the disabled and those with inadequate command
of official language(s).

248   We *recommend* that area offices should be established at
which all social security matters can be handled—on behalf

of different institutions in countries where unification cannot be
achieved (paragraph 164).

249 We *recommend* that social security institutions should
equip themselves to provide reasonably prompt answers
to reasonable inquiries from individuals about their personal entitlements, at area offices or in writing, and provide regular statements on accumulated rights to pensions where they exist (paragraph 166).

250 We *recommend* that organised systems of expert assistance
should be established to assist people to fill in applications
and to explain the contents of forms and letters; that social security
offices should all provide inquiry counters which are readily accessible to disabled people in wheelchairs; that communications
should be in Braille with blind people who have learnt to use it;
and that special measures should be taken for communication with
persons without an effective knowledge of the official language(s)
(paragraph 168).

251 We *recommend* that dispersed social security laws should
be integrated and possibly consolidated, and that the legislation should be drafted in the clearest possible language (paragraph
169).

252 We *recommend* that, in the absence of administrative
review by a judge or independent appeal board, one possibility is for complaints to be handled by an ombudsman (paragraph
171).

253 We *recommend* that all written notifications that a benefit
has been granted, refused or changed should include, in
simple language, an explanation of how and where to make a complaint and an appeal, and how to obtain legal or other help in
making it, free of charge (paragraph 173).

254   We *recommend* that it should be made illegal for social security institutions to reveal any information about individuals to third parties without their consent, unless specifically provided for in the law (paragraph 176).

255   We *recommend* that everyone should have access, under appropriate procedures, to their personal files in social security offices, the right to request changes, and the right to a fair hearing and prompt decision where they have a reasonable interest (paragraph 177).

256   We *recommend* that, where there is delay in establishing the precise level of a benefit, the claimant should be entitled to receive an advance and interest on any sum not paid on time. When an overpayment has been made, the beneficiary should be given reasonable time to repay (paragraph 178).

257   We *recommend* that social security institutions should widen the basis of participation in their advisory machinery and administration according to particular national situations (paragraph 180).

258   We *recommend* that each social security institution should be required to publish a comprehensive annual report on its administration, including a statement of income and expenditure in accordance with accepted accounting principles (paragraph 181).

The financing of social security

259   We find the argument that high employers' contributions are sharpening the world depression unconvincing. Nor do we believe that employers' contributions particularly damage labour-intensive firms. In so far as they do generally encourage more capital-intensive methods of production, this tends to increase international competitiveness. On the other hand, we believe that the presence of a relatively low ceiling on employers' contributions discourages part-time jobs by encouraging firms to prefer overtime

to taking on further employees and increases the relative cost of unskilled workers. This is damaging for employment. Apart from this, we do not see any compelling economic argument for choosing any particular method of financing social security. Thus the issue can be decided on social grounds.

260 We see the strongest case for financing by contributions where benefits are earnings-related and the strongest case for tax financing where it is desired to cover the whole resident population (e.g. for family allowances or health care). In general, we *recommend* progressive rather than regressive ways of financing social security. Partly for this reason, we believe that contribution ceilings for earnings-related benefits should be abolished. We *recommend* that a reasonable and appropriate portion of public contributory social security programmes be financed in part from the more progressive tax sources of the nation (paragraph 195).

261 What should be the role of the private sector in social security? The phrase "private sector" covers a whole range of different types of arrangements. We are in no doubt that subsidised non-profit voluntary associations can play an important role in providing particular types of services and should be encouraged. Moreover, there will be room for private supplementary insurance on top of statutory insurance to provide a higher level of protection or to meet special requirements of particular occupational groups. We *recommend* that means should be found of placing strict limits on tax concessions to such plans. The majority of us would go further and aim eventually to abolish them. At the very least, the majority *recommend* that the interest earned by non-governmental funds should be taxed (paragraph 198).

262 In the case of legal requirements for employers to provide directly limited parts of basic social security such as sick pay or redundancy payments, we see no objection, provided that the security granted is absolute. On balance, we do not generally favour placing of legal requirements on employers to provide social

security through private insurers, because of the high administrative costs, the introduction of risk rating which damages national solidarity, the risk of bankruptcy and the effects of competition in the case of occupational injury. We *recommend* that contracting out of public social security systems into private occupational pension plans should not be permitted (paragraph 203).

263   But what must be appreciated is that the use of the private sector does nothing to relieve the problem of tax resistance. Indeed, it may make it worse. People will still feel that they are not left with as much money as they want for their daily expenses.

264   The problem of tax resistance is central to current problems. It is essentially psychological and therefore becomes a matter for political decision. It is this that limits the level of contributions, rather than any economic considerations. The immediate so-called "crisis" has been caused above all else by lower rates of economic growth and heavy unemployment. It is grossly unfair to choose social security as the scapegoat and to ignore the growth of all other sectors of public expenditure and of private plans. In so far as there is a crisis in social security, it is not one of the structure of social security but of the erosion of the economic base for its operation. Social security is the cause of neither the crisis nor the recession.

*   *   *

265   The rate of economic growth will determine the rate at which progress can be made in the directions we have indicated. Careful choices will need to be made to achieve a balance within programmes and between programmes at each stage of development. In making these choices, those developments which benefit the poorest should have early attention.

266 Progress will not only depend on the developing economic situation. It will also depend on public awareness and appreciation of the fundamental principles underlying social security policies. The social change which is the aim of social security cannot be achieved if those who benefit from it do not play an active part in its development. It is essential for them to participate voluntarily in this process of change and to accept responsibility for the agencies created for them. In practice, for a variety of reasons, the consciousness of solidarity which should support all our efforts towards social security has tended to get weaker as the role of social security has widened. It is not possible to have social security, worthy of the name, without a consciousness of national solidarity and perhaps—tomorrow—international solidarity. The effort of developing social security must therefore be accompanied by a continuing effort to promote this crucial sense of shared responsibility.